# PRAISE FOR *THE FOUR PIVOTS*

"Reading this courageous book feels like the beginning of a social and personal awakening. By weaving together social science, storytelling, and his vast experience, Shawn explains why justice and healing are inextricably connected and how we can shift our thinking to create wholeness in our world and in ourselves. I can't stop thinking about it."

—BRENÉ BROWN, PhD, author of *Dare to Lead*

"Shawn Ginwright's book illuminates a needed path for our racially divided nation to move from a place of sobering pessimism toward what Dr. Martin Luther King, Jr. and John Lewis referred to as The Beloved Community. Ginwright thoughtfully unpacks this pathway as a staged journey, where each of us as individuals—and within the institutions we occupy—can translate one's lived experience into the sharing of story, human connectedness, and concerted action in service of full inclusion."

—ROBERT K. ROSS, MD, president and CEO
of The California Endowment

"Shawn Ginwright calls upon us to take four pivots that can enable us to engage in deep reflection about our actions and experiences so that we can lead happier, healthier, and more meaningful lives. . . . an invaluable resource for those who seek to grow, evolve, and make a difference in the world."

—PEDRO A. NOGUERA, PhD, Emery Stoops
and Joyce King Stoops Dean of the USC
Rossier School of Education

"*The Four Pivots* is a guide for those of us who believe loving toward racial justice is a worthy endeavor. It is a salve for those of us who know we cannot fight against the powerful forces maintaining racialized capitalism *without* seeding the ground with the dreams, joys, and promises of what we will become when we all belong. And it is a clarion call for movement leaders who know we need new ways of doing our work that replace exhaustion for laughter, uncertainty for curiosity, and rage for love."

—CARMEN ROJAS, PhD, president and CEO
of the Marguerite Casey Foundation

"This is a resource that will keep on giving. Shawn provides us with insight about our current selves and the current state of our struggle, then pivots us to see another world is possible! This is a hopeful guide to moving from internalized ways of being that are not serving us into transforming ourselves into collective coordination to envision and build our just new world."

—DENISE PERRY, director of BOLD (Black
Organizing for Leadership and Dignity)

"With wisdom, compassion and 'you feel me' humor, Shawn Ginwright invites us to care for and heal ourselves as we seek to care for and heal our world. A lifetime of stories and lessons learned— Ginwright's and others'—are distilled throughout the book and illuminate how so much of what we've been taught about social change work is wrong but also how we can make deeper shifts in our values on the path to real justice. Part guidebook and part manifesto, *The Four Pivots* offers a new architecture for future movement building. This is essential and vital reading for those committed to creating the world they imagine."

—CHERYL L. DORSEY, president of Echoing
Green Fellows

# The
# Four
# Pivots

*The*

# Four
# Pivots

## Reimagining Justice,
## Reimagining Ourselves

SHAWN A. GINWRIGHT, PhD

**North Atlantic Books**

Huichin, unceded Ohlone land
*aka* Berkeley, California

Published by
North Atlantic Books
Huichin, unceded Ohlone land
Berkeley, California

Cover art © Rayyy/Shutterstock.com
Cover design by Jess Morphew
Book design by Happenstance Type-O-Rama

Printed in the United States of America

*The Four Pivots: Reimagining Justice, Reimagining Ourselves* is sponsored and published by North Atlantic Books, an educational nonprofit based in the unceded Ohlone land Huichin (Berkeley, CA) that collaborates with partners to develop cross-cultural perspectives, nurture holistic views of art, science, the humanities, and healing, and seed personal and global transformation by publishing work on the relationship of body, spirit, and nature.

North Atlantic Books's publications are distributed to the US trade and internationally by Penguin Random House Publisher Services. For further information, visit our website at www.northatlanticbooks.com.

"Still I Rise" from *And Still I Rise*, copyright 1978 by Maya Angelou. Used by permission of Penguin Random House.

Library of Congress Cataloging-in-Publication Data
Names: Ginwright, Shawn A., author.
Title: The four pivots : reimagining justice, reimagining ourselves / Shawn A. Ginwright.
Description: Berkeley California : North Atlantic Books, [2021] | Includes bibliographical references. | Summary: "An activist's roadmap to long-term social justice impact through four simple shifts"—Provided by publisher.
Identifiers: LCCN 2021035125 (print) | LCCN 2021035126 (ebook) | ISBN 9781623175429 (trade paperback) | ISBN 9781623175436 (ebook)
Subjects: LCSH: Social justice—United States. | Equality—United States. | Social change—United States. | United States—Social conditions—21st century.
Classification: LCC HN59.2 .G545 2021 (print) | LCC HN59.2 (ebook) | DDC 303.3/72—dc23
LC record available at https://lccn.loc.gov/2021035125
LC ebook record available at https://lccn.loc.gov/2021035126

6 7 8 9 10 11 KPC 27 26 25 24 23

North Atlantic Books is committed to the protection of our environment. We print on recycled paper whenever possible and partner with printers who strive to use environmentally responsible practices.

*This book is dedicated to my father,
William Benjamin Ginwright Jr.,
affectionately known as "Poppa G."
Your love and light always guide
me through the wilderness of life.*

# CONTENTS

## *Pivot 1*
### FROM LENS TO MIRROR

## *Pivot 2*
### FROM TRANSACTIONAL TO TRANSFORMATIVE

## *Pivot 3*
### FROM PROBLEM TO POSSIBILITY

## *Pivot 4*
### FROM HUSTLE TO FLOW

# ACKNOWLEDGMENTS

The journey for this book began at the black kitchen table in my dining room. This is where my friends and family gather to enjoy wine, a great meal, and each other's company. More than anything, the black table is where wild ideas are born. One night over dinner and a few glasses of wine, I shared my idea for this book. Neither my friend and "baby sister" Jennifer Johns nor my wife, Nedra, was impressed by what I shared, and they pushed me to write something that was out of my comfort zone and spoke to a broader audience. They both challenged me to share what was really inside my head and heart and dared me to think beyond the confines of my professional and academic training. I'm not one to back down from a good dare, and this book would not have been possible without the rich conversations with Jennifer and Nedra. My family also dared me to integrate my life into the insights in this book. I'm forever grateful to my mother, Mae Ginwright, Aunt Sylvia Ginwright, Aunt Joyce Ballard, and my brothers, Chris and Graylin, whose love is tucked in between every word. My children, Takai and Nyah Ginwright, are artists and push my artistic limits, nudging me to unlock the artist within me. Thanks, kids, for teaching me, leading me, and showing me the power of a story well told. Writing a book is like embarking on a long uncertain journey. You might know the destination, but you're never precisely sure how to get there. Luckily, I've been blessed by many guides during my trip. David and Miko Hawkins (my brother and sister) reminded me of the responsibility to stay grounded, yet pushed me to fly. Dr. Macheo Payne and Marc Anthony Ellis are my intellectual pirates whose compass always points north no matter what storms may come.

I've been blessed with a mighty team of dreamers, doers, and pioneers who have shown me what it looks like to take flight. Thanks to everyone on the Flourish Agenda team. They lead me to the edge and, with a soft whisper, remind me that I have wings. Thank you, Dr. Denicia Carlay, for your painstaking review, edits, and comments. Your finger snaps, lols, and pointing out inconsistencies were invaluable. Dr. Vanessa Grubbs, you raised the bar for eloquence in writing; thanks for your early reviews. Deb Kersey worked hard on making sure to carve out time for me to write no matter how packed my calendar might have been. Dr. Julio Cammarota is more than a friend but also my intellectual soul mate whose life is an example combining scholarship and justice. Sai Seigel, your curious skepticism and feminist voice were always at the forefront of my thinking. Mia Haywood Jones, I'm grateful for our ride together, and you cleared the road and solved problems that I didn't even know were there. Dr. Christina "V" Villareal and Dr. Farima Pour-Khorshid, words cannot express how you have sharpened these ideas, deepened my thinking, and illuminated my life! The truth is, the black kitchen table belongs to all of us, and without Nedra none of these ideas would find root in our lives. Nedra, there is so much love you give, and I can only hope that this book will pour light into the lives of everyone who reads it, the same way you have done with so many others.

# INTRODUCTION

I used to think that my job as a professor was to teach. I had entered graduate school in 1994, eager to learn about educating students and improving schools. I was trained to read, research, contemplate, analyze, and write about all I had learned then impart knowledge to my eagerly awaiting students. I remember my first day as an assistant professor at Santa Clara University feeling completely insecure, overwhelmed, and over my head. I walked around the campus in fear that someone would find out that I had no idea what I was doing. My fear of being "found out" made me avoid talking to certain colleagues, determined how I enunciated my words, and influenced even how I dressed. If I could speak, dress, and behave like a professor, I thought, then no one would find out that I really wasn't. It was my secret, and I was determined to hide it from my students and colleagues at all costs. So I kept my secret safe, neatly tucked just beneath a fragile thin veneer of confidence I would muster up on my walks across campus.

Years later when I thought my fear had disappeared, it unexpectedly showed up again. During a graduate seminar, I began to notice how despondent and disconnected my students were to the material. When I asked them questions about the reading, they simply didn't respond. At first I thought it was because they hadn't read the material. After a few weeks of this, I abruptly stopped the class and straight out asked them why no one had read the material.

One student replied, "Dr. Ginwright, did you actually read your own syllabus?"

I was puzzled and replied with confidence, "Of course I've read the syllabus, I designed this course." I was somewhat perturbed by her question.

Yet another student commented, "Did you review *all* of the syllabus?" By now I knew something was wrong, so I glanced down at the title of my syllabus—it read "African American Social Theory Spring 2007." The class I was teaching was in the fall of 2012.

I was mortified that I had failed to update the readings and revise the materials for timely and relevant examples. Immediately my fear, the one that I thought had somehow disappeared, showed up and was staring me right in the face. So I did what any insecure, fear-filled professor would do—I lied to save face. I replied in my confident, proper, deep professor voice, "Well, the theoretical underpinnings of sociological phenomena remain in Black life and these readings, while dated, are classic and still relevant to . . . blah, blah, blah . . ." They could see that I was bullshitting and hiding from them the truth, which was simply that I had majorly fucked up.

After escaping the embarrassment of this moment, I had two decisions to make. I could use my position and power as a professor to sweep my mistake under the rug, or I could come clean and tell the truth. I chose the latter, to tell the truth. The following week, after deep reflection and contemplation, I came into class and had an honest conversation about my mistake. I admitted that I hadn't been as organized and thoughtful about the course as I should have been. I didn't make excuses, but I explained that I was tired. Not the kind of tired you can just sleep off and wake up the next day and be cool. Naw, I was tired down to the roots, at my core. I was tired of meaningless meetings, tired of constantly raising money for my work, tired of not knowing where I was going in life. I apologized to them from my gut, because I really value my students' learning. I didn't just mimic the words "I'm sorry" or "my bad." I was truly regretful, and they knew it, they could feel me. You feel me?

That conversation transformed the class, and my relationships with my students, in ways that I could not imagine. I suspect that somewhere in that clumsy apology they stopped seeing me as Professor Ginwright and began to see me as fully human. I imagine that in me standing in front of the class, somewhere in my stumbling over words, they saw something familiar, something they could relate to—my imperfection. They trusted what I said because it was real, no theoretical underpinning, no framework, no philosophical point, no bullshit, just damn honest. I said to them, "I messed up, I hope to regain your trust, I'm gonna do better." I suppose that my being honest and vulnerable allowed me to let go of my fear, and in doing so opened something in us that connected us beyond the confines of teacher and student. For the rest of our semester together, we played, laughed, cried, and relished in simply being human; we healed.

I think that much of what we know about healing is wrong. Well, not entirely wrong, but rather incomplete. For most of my career, as an advocate for youth, nonprofit leader, and professor, I've thought about healing as a process focused on fixing harms and/or repairing wounds inflicted by oppression and structural inequality. But I've come to realize that as a society, we don't really do a good job at preparing, teaching, or training people how to be vulnerable, cultivate empathy, practice self-reflection—all the stuff that makes us human. Healing involves more than repairing the deep wounds of racism, healing the scars of sexism, or easing the pains of poverty. Healing is the capacity to restore our humanity and care for ourselves and others even in the midst of our fear. Healing is the only pathway to real justice because it requires that we take an honest look at what harmed us and pushes us to restore our humanity and finally to move us confidently into a possible future.

While my training as a graduate student at UC Berkeley prepared me with deep analysis of our social problems, I wasn't given the tools to deal with my own trauma, fears, and insecurities. I believed that my analysis of social problems was enough to change them. But I was wrong. Of course, I didn't know I was wrong thirty years ago when I founded an organization that focused on training thousands of Black youth to analyze social problems, build power, and change their schools and communities. Since that time, I've learned that changing things that are broken in our society requires individual and collective healing. I've learned from young people, their families, and community partners all the lessons that were missing from my graduate school training. They have taught me that the most important aspect of social change is not problem analysis, power building, narrative change, or coalition building—it's healing.

The regularity of mass shootings, innocent citizens gunned down by police, urban youth violence, and rural opioid use among youth all have one thing in common: they are symptoms of a society that is broken. Americans are more depressed, commit suicide more frequently, and have little hope in the future, and our leaders have no idea what to do about it. America's capitalist culture based in individualism, fear, and scarcity is toxic and has taken a toll on how we work, live, and relate to one another. We can feel it when we go to work, we can see it when we turn on the television, and we can hear it when we listen to the news. The solutions to these challenges won't be found through progressive or conservative politics; a deeper shift is needed in our values and our ability to heal from the wounds of racism, sexism, and poverty.

I sometimes think we grossly underestimate how inequality impacts us. I'm not talking about inequality in the sense of wage gaps, unemployment, or access to quality health care. I think we all are familiar with all the evidence from research about these types of inequality. I'm more curious about the less obvious ways that inequality impacts us: how inequality erodes hope, shatters dreams, and breeds othering. Imagine if your home had asbestos and lead paint everywhere. In addition to that, you lived next to a factory that spewed toxic fumes into the air. Over time, these toxins would eventually have an impact on your health and well-being. You might develop a slight but stubborn cough that won't go away. Your slight cough then turns into a nasty chest infection that ultimately begins to weaken your breathing and so on. Y'all get the picture, that's what inequality does to us—it slowly erodes away at our collective well-being, and its symptoms can be seen in how we relate to one another.

Take for example call-out or cancel culture. Call-out culture boils down to publicly shaming individuals (usually on social media) for behavior or statements that are perceived as noninclusive and oppressive. The tendency is to attack the perpetrator for not being woke, and the act of public shaming or calling out is seen as a form of political activism in itself. Yet at the same time call-out culture serves an important function for those of us who have been rendered invisible, violently silenced, and callously ignored when speaking out against gender violence, racial harm, and inhumane treatment. The #MeToo movement remains one of the most significant and powerful movements of our time by breaking the silence and shame associated with violence, sexual harassment, and abuse against vulnerable individuals. The movement empowers individuals who have experienced sexual assault to hold perpetrators accountable for their actions.

The question for us isn't simply, Is call-out culture good or bad? Rather, the question is, Are we devolving or evolving in our collective capacity to engage in conflicting ideas and conflict itself? This is the central question that Loretta Ross, professor at Smith College, challenges social justice advocates to wrestle with.[1] How do we discern when to hold someone accountable and when to deploy grace? How do we learn to elegantly dance between the two? These questions ultimately will advance our discourse and movements in transformative ways.

I remember being called out in public during a large workshop I was conducting with a roomful of about 200 graduate students, faculty, and activists from around the country. One of the activities during the session required people to mingle with each other to break the ice. After the icebreaker, I instructed people to pair up with a complete stranger, and they were asked to respond to a series of thought-provoking questions that made them dig deep. I've done this activity over 1,000 times, and generally people respond favorably to the activity because it creates space for deep reflection.

After the activity during the question-and-answer segment, a middle-aged, well-dressed white woman stood up and commenced to call me out for not being inclusive. Her hair was graying, and when she stood up, she spoke with confidence without hesitation. "This was the most noninclusive activity I've ever seen, because it favored physically able people and completely discounted people without hearing or sight," she explained passionately. How is this healing "when you're promoting oppressive activities that harm so many people?" The woman was in a roomful of BIPOC (Black, Indigenous, People of Color) activists and it was obvious to me that her intent was to demonstrate to the room her "wokeness" because as she spoke, her eyes searched the audience to catch nods of agreement and applause.

I didn't know how to respond except to say that I was not perfect, neither was the activity we had just experienced. I explained from a place of humility that my intent was to explore how we could cultivate more transformative relationships in our movement work. The truth is, she was correct. I hadn't considered how the activity reinforced ableist practices and language, yet at the same time I felt attacked. It was a reflective learning moment, and it revealed areas in my work that were hidden from me. Shortly after my comments to the group, an African American woman in her early thirties stood up and explained that the white woman's comments were another demonstration of white fragility and white supremacy. She wore a sweatshirt with the name of her graduate school, but the name was covered by her long braids that flowed over her shoulders. The room was mostly women of color who deeply appreciated the opportunity to share and "go deep" with each other. The white woman's comments, from the Black woman's perspective, failed to appreciate the sacred space that was created.

I realized that call-out culture is simply a symbol of a deeper trauma. We are all wounded and carry the shame and pain in ways that we are unaware of, and as a result we sometimes harm others. Yet we are not equipped with the skills or the awareness to heal our trauma.

Perhaps the white woman's comments were fueled by a need to feel accepted by women of color because of unhealed rejection she may have experienced with folks of color. Inequality, in all its forms, doesn't only block opportunities, it also breeds individualism, distrust, skepticism, and fear. These powerful forces show up in our movements, systems-change efforts, and communities, yet we simply don't have the tools to name or heal from these symptoms caused by exposure to inequality.

Another example is how community leaders sometimes believe that they are the only ones doing the "real work" while other organizations are just "collecting checks" without delivering much impact. While there may be some truth to this skepticism, it comes without a deeper understanding of the ways that philanthropy sometimes breeds conflict among groups over funding. Groups compete over resources without much power to determine how funding should be structured in the first place. Again, inequality is toxic and breeds deeper psychosocial wounds that are like obstruction spots for us— we can't always see how they impact our efforts to change our society.

The bottom line is that we all have these obstruction spots that make it difficult to connect with each other in meaningful ways. These obstruction spots also make it difficult for us to cultivate a vision of the world we really want to live in. Most of our work is focused on eliminating those things that cause us harm. Addressing racism, fighting sexism, and reducing violence are all important, but reductions in these things are not victories in and of themselves because eliminating things that harm us is not the same as creating things that heal us. Just like the absence of disease doesn't constitute health, nor does the absence of violence constitute peace, simply ending these problems does little to cultivate the world we really want. But that is how inequality works! Inequality erodes our ability to imagine any other way, and it conditions us to only focus on surface solutions to deep problems. It predefines our dreams and dictates what we can imagine. That's why so many of us have a hard time describing what freedom feels, looks, smells, and sounds like. We haven't spent much time with that type of question and sometimes find it difficult to visualize a world we want to create. We spend all of our time *resisting* white supremacy, *fighting* racism, *confronting* patriarchy, *deconstructing* capitalism, *challenging* oppressive systems, and very little time *creating* belonging, *cultivating* healing, *inventing* new systems, *designing* our future.

Somewhere along the way we all have bought into the myth that working harder for justice, removing barriers to inequality, and deeply analyzing policies are enough to transform our society. These are myths because working harder, removing barriers, and analyzing policies simply don't get at the deeper, more fundamental issues that plague our movements for justice. Trust, vision, wholeness, humane relationships, and hope are the real lifeline of movement building. This means working on self-transformation, healing, hopefulness, and cultivating a vision of possibility. Yet these spaces do not exist in our work as we now know it. As a result, this absence has been the Achilles' heel of our efforts to engage in social change in a deeper way. Here are a few lies about social change that I want to highlight.

## THE FOUR LIES ABOUT SOCIAL CHANGE

### Lie 1: Deep Change Can Be Achieved through Shallow Solutions

I've heard from policy makers, educational leaders, social justice advocates, and community organizers that all that really matters in creating the society we want is that we remove the barriers to fairness. Employment inequality, gender discrimination, and racist housing policies are indeed barriers, and their removal is important to improve the quality of life for communities. This myth is not meant to discount the efforts of folks who tirelessly work to improve the structural impediments to equitable health care, housing, jobs, and police accountability.

A conversation comes to mind from a retreat where an organizer who worked to increase Black voting power in rural America explained to me that "healing doesn't really matter if we don't all have opportunities and access to livable wages, health care, and education." Her point was that the concept of healing didn't mean much if folks were still suffering. I agree, removing structural barriers is important. Removing the barriers does very little, however, to restore the harm and injury to communities caused by inequality. For instance, waiving the application fees for college will remove a financial barrier, allowing more candidates to apply, but it won't change the fact that under-resourced high schools are unable to prepare their students for the college application process in the same way that affluent schools are.

The myth is that deep change can be achieved by shallow solutions. By *shallow* I don't mean trivial or insignificant. What I mean is that our solutions rarely engage the root of the problems we are trying to solve. Fear, scarcity, division, distrust, isolation—all are at the root of many of the world's problems. Rather than trying to heal fear, scarcity, division, distrust, and isolation, which is really hard, we choose instead to address the symptoms of these more fundamental problems. We can address racist policies but never address the xenophobic fear that created it. We can respond to gender inequality but leave unscathed the toxic masculinity that created it. When we focus on solving surface problems, it's like we are playing the game whack-a-mole because we are always waiting to respond to the next problem that shows up.

I feel like that whenever a Black boy is killed by a cop, or a high school kid shoots up their school, or a gunman opens fire on a crowd of innocent people. When I read the story or watch the news, I take a deep breath and silently say to myself, "Shit, not again!" Then I shake my head in a sort of manufactured disbelief and try to find a reason why it happened. Maybe it was the police officer's racist anxiety and fear of Black people that led them to unintentionally shoot the victim; maybe the kid was being bullied at school, and no one listened to them. But the truth is that we have become too comfortable with surface solutions to really deep problems.

For example, I understand why our communities have advocated for policies for police officers to wear body cameras. The thinking is that officers act better when they know they are being recorded. Early research shows some evidence of this practice reducing officers' use of force and citizen complaints,[2] but I'm worried that body cameras are just a surface solution to a deeper issue. Body cameras don't train police in anti-racist behavior, and they fail to address racial fear and anxiety officers hold about Black people and our communities. Body cameras don't require police officers to unpack and reflect on their subconscious biases. Deep change in policing and community safety will require us to rethink policing as we know it. You might be thinking, "How will my self-healing get the police to do deep change? Isn't incremental change better than just sitting here waiting for everybody to heal?" These are questions that I'll address later, but for now we have to first see how these myths force us to solve the wrong problems and lock into ways of thinking that don't always get at the root of the problems we need to solve.

## Lie 2: The More Power We Have, the More Change We Can Create

For years I have worked with community organizations and young people and have focused on building power. I've written extensively about the power of youth organizing and why this form of power building is necessary to create the type of changes we need for BIPOC young people. What I have learned over the years is that I've been thinking about power as a collective force attained from withholding labor, boycotting, or raising awareness about an issue in order to achieve some desired goal or objective. We knock on doors of our neighbors so that they can join the neighborhood effort to make our schools better. We join together in protest and march to make the police accountable for their actions. We write blogs to raise awareness about climate change. We vote for candidates who we think will represent our best interest in local and national government. All these efforts are directed at building power to shift things for the better.

But there's one problem with this form of power building that folks rarely acknowledge. It rarely addresses our collective trauma or our individual healing. Power is not only the collective capacity to influence resources and policy. Power is also an "inside job" that comes from our collective convictions that we discover when we imagine together and heal our own insecurities and fears.

This myth about power is not one to be taken lightly, and I know some of y'all will point to examples where activists and community leaders have organized and garnered collective power to force, fight for, and demand a desired policy or reallocation of resources. This form of collective power may lead to important changes in opportunities, but how do we account for the physical and emotional toll this form of organizing has on individuals? How does power come from us turning inward and focusing on our own healing? What does healing have to do with social change? Well, sometimes we use our activism as an excuse to avoid the real stuff that is happening in our lives. We have the tendency to work outwardly in helping a young person repair their relationship with their father but refuse to do our own work in repairing the relationship we have with our own father. We focus on building the organization instead of building healthy relationships in our own family. We organize our communities instead of addressing our addiction to alcohol.

Activism and our efforts for collective power become like a substitute for turning inward because turning inward is way too scary and messy. Dealing with our addictions, insecurities, and unresolved conflicts is way harder than making people aware of the dangers of climate change or fighting against racist policies. But when we don't turn inward to deal with our own stuff, we build up this false idea about power and ultimately build movements with wounded warriors. Our real power comes from the courage to deal with our fractured relationships, the vulnerability to acknowledge our hurt feelings, and the awareness to know when our ego shows up.

## Lie 3: We Can Strategize Solutions for Social Change

Every year during the fall or spring semester I'll have a conversation with one of my graduate students about their future. They'll sit on the blue couch in my office while I finish grading papers, send off a few emails, and try to organize the clutter of student papers on my desk. Our conversations usually begin with "Dr. G, I think I want to go to law school after I graduate" or "Dr. G, what type of job should I get after I graduate?"

I always respond with the same question, "What do you *want* to do—if you could imagine the dream scenario, what would that be?" Even after all these years, I'm surprised by the response I usually get. Generally, my students have no idea how to answer the question, and instead they dive headfirst into a monologue about getting a job, earning money, and what their parents told them they should do after graduating.

Most of the time, though, my students are clearer about what they don't want than what they actually desire. They know they don't want to go back home after experiencing the newly found freedom of being on their own, they don't want to waste time in college because of the cost of tuition, they don't want to work for a large company where they can't express their individuality, they don't want to fail and disappoint their parents. In fact, in most cases my students don't really indulge themselves in dreaming about what they want and instead just want a good map detailing what they should do, without a clear destination of where they want to go. They want a precise map to a vague destination.

The lie we tell ourselves is that if our maps are clear and precise, then we can solve the problems of income inequality, climate change, and structural racism. Our work at social change has become an effort to make better maps without a clear, compelling destination. It doesn't matter how good your map is without a clear and compelling destination. The focus on creating the perfect strategy leads to a sort of way of thinking that we can engineer solutions to deep change. By *strategizing solutions* I mean the mechanistic and technical application of data, information, and plans to solve intractable social problems.

For example, I remember working with a division of a large city government. They wanted me to support them with building equity in their systems and design ways to train their workforce in healing-centered strategies. My team quickly learned that the city division viewed racial inequality and exposure to trauma in the city entirely through the lens of sophisticated population data. If $x$ population has $y$ exposure to trauma, then the solution should involve higher doses of $z$! They were reaching for just the right evidence-based solution supported with data. The social issue (racial inequality and trauma exposure) was sort of viewed as a calculus problem, and the levels of bureaucracy in the division created a technical and mechanistic way of thinking about efficiency, order, redundancy, inputs, and outputs. The division's leaders were largely removed from the issues they wanted to solve, and they wanted my team to engineer a solution rather than work with the community to discover one.

There are hundreds of other examples like this, but the point is that social change (to borrow a term from adrienne maree brown) is emergent. That is, leaders need to get closer to the problem, not further away, in order to cultivate a compassionate curiosity about how to work toward a solution in partnership with communities. This type of work toward social changes takes time, efficacy, trust, skepticism, resources, scarcity, uncertainty, thinking, dreaming, relationship, confusion, clarity, frustration, work, play, analysis, and spirit. Yes, it takes leaning into the full range of our human experience that allows us to cultivate a sense of urgent faith that our collective leaning-in will yield just what we need.

## Lie 4: Us versus Them

Check it: My momma always dreamed of living in a big nice home. She was raised in Jacksonville, Florida, and her father worked at Winn-Dixie grocery for minimum wage. With her sister and brother (my aunt and uncle), they all lived in a small house made of cinder block in a row of houses that lined a sewage canal. Their home was small but clean and quaint. So when my father and mother moved from Florida to Riverside, California, they settled into a modest home in a neighborhood at the bottom of a hill just beneath a lavish housing development. Growing up, we would play in the large dirt field that separated our neighborhood from the white folks that lived in the homes at the top of the hill. The summers in Riverside were hot, and we would spend our days making clubhouses in the trees, collecting lizards from underneath rocks, and playing with our Hot Wheels in our imaginary homes made of sand, sticks, mud, and whatever we could find.

We didn't think much about the fact that we were poor, except that the white people that lived on the hill had swimming pools, manicured front lawns, and well-kept, neatly parked cars in the driveway. I suppose that is where my momma began dreaming about living in a big house. She would say, "Lawd-ha-mercy, Linda got a big house! And it's so nice . . ." She always compared her modest home to her friends' and other white folks'. For her, *we* were the ones with small homes; *they* were the ones with big ones. It was two clear worlds.

I'm not sure when I began to see the world as us versus them, but I think it somehow began with those white folks in those big homes. We, or "us," were the ones at the bottom of the hill wishing we had swimming pools to play in during the hot summers. They, or "them," were the ones that looked down at us from their homes, took vacations, and went out to dinner whenever they wanted to. We/us were the ones who wished we could.

We see the world as us versus them, and it's hard not to. Our history and our lives remind us every day which groups we belong to and which groups we don't. In fact, research shows that humans are wired for this. Anthropologists and primatologists have observed that us versus them exists in the natural world and has contributed to human survival. Psychologists have studied how we tend to associate positive attributes to our "us" group and assign negative attributes to "them." Just think for a moment of social identity groups with whom you most identify. Black, white, Latinx, gay, single, Green Party, New Yorker, environmentalist, entrepreneur, it doesn't matter. Chances are that you view this "us" group in generally favorable terms. Now think for a moment about a group with whom you least identify. Again, chances are the thought of spending a week with the latter group frightens you!

Even though this is a natural human tendency to see the world as us versus them, it's a myth for two reasons. First, the criteria we use to determine the groups we belong to generally obscure the more essential elements of what it means to be human. In other words, we identify and assign meaning to aspects of our identities that we hold on to so tightly that they prevent us from cultivating empathy and connection with folks outside our identity groups. Now I know y'all thinking, "WTF! How am I supposed to develop empathy for the elite and wealthy, or try to understand the perspective of a white supremacist?" But those are the wrong questions. The real question is, How do I cultivate the ability to still see the humanity in those whom I vehemently disagree with? This is perhaps one of the most difficult myths for us to swallow given the ongoing history of dehumanization and violence in our communities.

The danger, however, is that us-and-them thinking ultimately leads to *othering*, the process of labeling groups of people with negative attributes and then identifying with the positive attributes of your own group. This process ultimately draws thick and hard boundaries about who is human and who is not. Us-versus-them thinking is precisely what created slavery, Jim Crow racism, the lynching of Africans, the genocide of Native Americans, and a legacy of dehumanization. Us versus them is a deeply colonized way of thinking because it is the root of the white supremacist thinking that created the conditions for dehumanization of so many people.

*Belonging* is the capacity to see the humanity in those that are not like us and to recognize that the same elements that exist within them also exist within us. It means that we have to see the humanity in others, even if they refuse to see the same in us. Yeah, belonging is really hard work, and the capacity to see the humanity in those that are not like us is perhaps one of the most powerful practices we need to cultivate. It is a way of constructing an imagined connection, a kinship, an identity that allows us to make sense of the world that is both real and imagined. But it requires that we see the myth in us versus them.

Reinventing revolution and bringing love into social change is what Grace Lee Boggs called it. Cultivating a "beloved community" is what Dr. King called it. The idea that we can create within ourselves, our movements, and our work a deeper sense of connection, or empathy, is powerful because it forces us into leaning into new possibilities, different ways of relating, alternative ways of connecting. No human is intrinsically better or worse than the next. While it's true that the conditions of our lives are different, we should be careful not to confuse the quality of conditions of a human with the quality of the human themselves. We are all flawed—and trying desperately to hide it. The truth is that the quality of our journey is not figuring out how to be perfect but rather reflecting on who we become in the process. The process of healing is often counter to our common sense. More loving when we are hated, more generous in times of scarcity, more inclusive when we want to close ranks. This is the greatest challenge in our journey toward justice.

## A PIVOT TOWARD HEALING

So how do we let go of these myths and embrace an alternative set of truths that can guide our work and our lives? Letting go of myths is not easy because it means that we have to admit to ourselves that the stories we live by simply aren't true. But I guess that's the first step, realizing that the stories we've believed in don't really work anymore, and that may be a hard pill to swallow, especially when these stories have survived the toxic environments we find ourselves in. But when we do this, we begin to heal ourselves and our communities. The bottom line is, when we let go of these myths, we begin to embrace a healing-centered way of life. We are all trying to figure out ways to live, work, and play while making the world better.

We need a fundamental shift in our values, a pivot in how we think, connect, act, and work. A *pivot* is a small change in direction from a single point where we are. It means that through one small change in direction, over time we can get to where we want to be. A pivot is not a complete abandonment of what we know, but it braids together what we know with how we feel and who we wish to be. For example, in basketball a pivot requires four interwoven and seamless traits. When a player has the ball, they pivot in order to advance the ball down the court. This pivot requires that (1) they stop momentarily and reflect on what is happening, (2) they have awareness of the relationships of other players around them, (3) they maintain focus on the goal without distraction, and (4) they calmly and confidently flow into another direction. You don't see all of this of course because it all happens in an instant.

That's what we need as individuals, as communities, and as a society. A pivot acknowledges collective harm and individual injury but also leans into the future and opens entirely new possibilities. A pivot involves renewing our sense of possibility, transforming how we see the world, and shifting the values of our culture. This can only happen when we foster a collective imagination that restores communal wisdom that embraces both imagination and engagement, empathy and power, reflection and action. A pivot means that we need to dream higher about the future we want to create.

This book is about the pivots we need to make as individuals, as communities, and as a society. I've come to know these pivots both professionally in my work with organizations and communities and personally in raising two beautiful children, in my relationship with my wife of nearly thirty years, and in my relationships with close friends. Just to keep it real, I struggle with these pivots and don't claim that they come easy to me. I don't want you to think that I walk through the world as an example of how to live, work, and play using the pivots that will guide your journey through this book. I do want you to know that perfection (living in our perfect pivots) is not the goal in my writing this book. Rather, it's a commitment to an imperfect journey.

Your journey in this book is composed of four pivots. The first section focuses on the pivot in our **awareness: from lens to mirror**. Instead of viewing the world through a thick lens—that is, as analysts of social problems—we must view it as a mirror of ourselves. This involves the practice of self-reflection and exploration of who we are as individuals and how we contribute to the world we wish to create. The second section is dedicated to a pivot in our **connection: from transactional to transformative relationships**. Most of us have been trained to lead and work with others in highly technical ways. Transactional relationships are efficient for work and productivity but insufficient for healing. Transformative relationships in our professional and personal lives cultivate deeper human connection through vulnerability, empathy, and listening. The third section highlights a pivot in **vision: from problem fixing to possibility creating**. As I discussed earlier, the history of exclusion, a scarcity mindset, and zero-sum thinking resulting from inequality come with a psychic cost. We have been socialized to focus on fixing problems and not on creating entirely new possibilities. The last section is committed to a pivot in **presence: from hustle to flow**. This involves transforming our addiction to frenzy, which is one toxic result of our capitalist culture, to an existence of calm well-being. We all know what it feels like to be addicted to frenzy, whether we love staying busy or have to hustle for survival. We are always busy, behind on pesky tasks, overcommitted, and in a rush to the next meeting or event. If we can admit it to ourselves, we know deep down that we get a great deal of satisfaction from our addiction to frenzy. This is because we say to ourselves, "If I'm busy, I'm important and I matter." Like any addiction, however, this gratification obscures the core truth: that our addiction to frenzy gets in the way of our healing and well-being. A shift to well-being means we reclaim our right to be well. We slow down the pace of our day, we say no more often and without guilt, and we take a nap every now and then!

At the end of each section, you'll have an opportunity to do some work. I've included a few activities and lessons that can support you in making these pivots. Think of these activities as guardrails that help you along the path and steer you in the right direction. I've included these activities because so many times I've heard the questions "What do I do? And how do I use these pivots?" These lessons are meant for you to practice, practice, practice and discover how these pivots can make a difference in your work and life. They are also designed to push, nudge, and cajole a new way of thinking about work, relationships, and social change. I suggest that you read this with your colleagues at work or your friends to share what you are learning. I hope that by practicing ways to reflect, create belonging, cultivate vision, and foster empathy, we can build the momentum we need to ultimately transform our culture.

# Pivot 1

## From Lens to Mirror

# 1

# *Reflection*

*Mirror, mirror, on the wall,*
*who's the wokest of them all?*

grew up on Walter Street. It was a boring name for a street, but my summers were exciting and filled with playing outside until the streetlights came on. Then when the streetlights came on, my brothers and I would squeeze out just a few more games of tag or Marco Polo before Momma would call us home. Naw, not on a cell phone, but call us like yell from behind the screen door . . . "Hey boys, bring y'all narrow butts home, don't let me have to tell you again!" Our house on Walter Street had green shag carpet, and in the kitchen Moms kept a large coffee can near the stove where she would pour the extra bacon, fish, or Spam grease after cooking. We couldn't play in the living room where her nice furniture was on display. She protected the living room with plastic covers over the couch and loveseat, and a plastic runner in the hallway led us to the forbidden room. You know those plastic covers that obscured and protected the full beauty of the valuable items underneath them.

The cover would make a crinkling sound when you sat on it and stick to you once you started sweating. In the forbidden room, Pops had a wood-grain hi-fi (high fidelity) stereo where we would sneak to listen to Richard Pryor albums when they went out with their friends. The two speakers connected to the hi-fi system were used like end tables, one on each side of the couch, where two green glass ashtrays rested.

My mother had gone to a department store and fallen in love with a large mirror that she thought would be perfect above the couch. The mirror was framed in golden leaves that reminded me of a Roman artwork. In 1973 she walked into Barker Brothers department store and purchased this mirror that would find its home in my momma's living room to this very day. She placed the mirror right above the couch, the one covered with plastic, and for nearly fifty years this mirror has witnessed every moment of our family's growth. Like the time when my baby brother ran into the house after he set the backyard fence on fire. He ran right past the mirror, into our room, and underneath his bed. The mirror saw everything. Or the time when my father ran out of lighter fluid for the big backyard barbeque he had been preparing for all week. Instead of going to the store to pick up more lighter fluid, he soaked the black Kingsford charcoal with gasoline from the lawn mower's gas can. My friends and I stood back and watched him light the grill, and *boooom*—it exploded in his face! That's when he ran to the mirror, the one above the couch in the living room, to see the damage. Luckily, he had only singed his eyebrows, and his face and his body were covered with black soot. My momma didn't care much about the explosion; she just wanted him out of the living room to keep all that soot off her good furniture.

Easter Sundays were the best. My brothers and I would get all dressed up and pose in front of the mirror in our clothes that Moms and Pops had just gotten out of layaway. We would stand in front of that mirror to shape, pat, pick, and pat again our Afros into round Black perfection. That mirror has seen countless hours of me practicing the moonwalk, the cabbage patch, the wap, the gigolo, and my best Run-DMC hip-hop poses. It has also seen each of us run away from home, argue, laugh, cry, fight, drink, smoke, play cards, date, and break up. It has watched me in shags, Jheri curls, high top fades, and locks, all without judgment, but always telling me the truth.

I guess that's what all good mirrors have been hired to do. It's their job to reflect back at us the honest truth without judgment. That's why we hire them into our families and assign their duties to our bathrooms, have them work night and day in our bedrooms, and require their endless labor in hallways with plastic runners.

Mirrors, if you hire a good one, for the most part tell the truth and reflect back the hardcore reality that you've been hiding from. Sometimes we need a good mirror to remind us when we are fooling ourselves into thinking that the outfit we just bought fits or is cute. We use mirrors to show us what's hard to see, like our own faces. We use mirrors to help us cover up blemishes, shave, and put on makeup. Mirrors were made for truth-telling, and they do this eloquent job with grace, without complaint, and for very little pay.

Sometimes, though, mirrors get disgruntled and reject the truth-telling assignment that we give them. That's when they distort and bend the truth just enough to fool us that what we see before us, the reflection, is in fact true. Most of these mirrors, the disgruntled ones, are forced to work in carnivals or amusement parks, where twisting the truth, bending honesty, and misconstruing clarity are for our entertainment. Fortunately, these mirrors don't find themselves working in our homes mostly because we expect that when we walk in front of one, they will do their job and reflect back the truth that's hard for us to see.

If our mirrors could talk to us, we'd learn a lot about who we are. They would tell us what motivates us and what we fear most. They would explain to us, without hesitation, what irritates us and what makes us feel insecure. If we were to press our faces real close to the mirror and listen, sometimes they would surprise us with something we didn't even know. Like finding a bump on your chin, it's been there for a while, you just didn't take the time to really see it.

\* \* \*

Most of us walk through the world with very little self-reflection. Either we just don't have the time, or we don't see the value in self-reflection. As a result, we just don't see what the mirror is trying to tell us because somewhere along the way we were told to see the world through a lens—an outwardly focused explanation, precise analysis, external diagnosis, and rigid framework about how the world works. As a trained sociologist, I've also been guilty of this process. I was trained to study, examine, analyze, and investigate social problems, and I was given all the necessary theories to do so. While my lenses were useful in exploring outwardly focused social problems, they never once forced me to examine myself. A lens defines what we see even before we see it. A lens is an outwardly focused examination about how the world works, and for the most part it helps us explain social issues that would otherwise be considered "natural." Take for instance the fact that men earn more than women, or the fact that there is a significant wealth gap between Blacks and whites. Without a good lens, our explanations of these issues would be based on myth, not science. For example, we might believe the myth that white people work harder than Black people or that women are not as competent in the workforce as men if we didn't have science prove otherwise. A lens also helps illuminate complex answers to hidden social phenomena that aren't easily explained.

But our lenses over time can also create obstruction spots, because lenses are awful at reflecting back the truth about ourselves. It's easy to identify and examine the external impact of racism because we see it everywhere. We see racism at work, on the news, in our neighborhoods, at the mall, and in our schools. While our lenses help us see and unpack the impact of racism on racial and ethnic groups, it's much harder to reflect on what happens inside us when we experience it. Our lenses help us explain and understand how sexism, homophobia, or patriarchy works, but they completely fail at exploring shame and hurt when we experience it.

## BLACK MEN AND MIRRORS

As a Black man, I struggle with when to use my lens and when to stare into my mirror. I walk through the world always aware that, despite my middle-class status, racism will show up. When it does show up, what surprises me most about racism is that I'm surprised at all. Like the time when my friends and I were politely asked to leave a well-known restaurant in Oakland, California. It went down like this. My boys wanted to take me out to dinner and drinks to celebrate my birthday. Instead of making a beeline to our favorite watering hole, we decided to check out another restaurant downtown. One of my boys, Macheo, had just purchased a Tesla, and I was in the passenger's seat playing with the iPad-looking screen console like a kid on Christmas morning. Now, I know we aren't in our twenties anymore, but I couldn't help it. I turned up the volume—way up—to feel the pulsating, booming bass from the subwoofers when Too Short's "Blow the Whistle" came on. Ahhh yeah, we was feeling ourselves, and it was gonna be a great birthday celebration.

When we arrived at the restaurant, we saw that there were plenty of open tables. The hostess must have felt us coming in, four Black men, all six feet tall and feeling ourselves. That's when she asked if we wanted a table. "Sure, we'd like a table for four," my friend said.

The hostess replied, "OK, well, if you get a table you need to spend a minimum of twenty dollars per person, but the bar is open and you can sit anywhere at the bar if you would like."

Umm, let me grab my lens; I need to know what the hell is going on here. This was a clear attempt, my lens told me, to keep the riff-raff out of the establishment and only appeal to the newly arrived white gentrifiers.

My boy Marc wasn't having it; he replied, "Hey, do you ask everybody this? What makes you think we wouldn't spend at least twenty dollars, and why—"

Before he could finish his sentence, she walked off and returned with an older woman, who I figured would quickly resolve this matter, but she just doubled down. "In order to get a table, you need to spend at least twenty dollars per person, or maybe you all should just sit at the bar. As a matter of fact, we're not going to serve you. You all need to leave or I'll call the police."

There it is again, my lens, or wait . . . should I use my mirror? My lens offered me the perfect clarity about what was happening, good ole-fashion in-your-face racism in The Town. My mirror also allowed me to reflect on what was going on inside my heart. I was furious, angry, embarrassed, and resentful that this shit was happening to us and all we could do was leave.

* * *

But leaving isn't always an option, particularly when there's nowhere to go. Take for instance enslaved Africans in the Americas, who suffered unimaginable brutality and unthinkable psychic pain from families being torn apart. It wasn't easy to just get up and leave the South's lynchings, debt bondage, and Jim Crow reality. When Black families did migrate north, they continued to face discrimination, anger, humiliation, and fear. Most families were focused on the future and were working to pave a way for a better way of life. Reflecting on the past, the hurt, and pain and trauma was just too painful, so we buried it. There was no need to deal with the hurtful, shameful past, so we just kept it moving and kept on surviving. With every generation our secrets, hurt, shame, and disappointment keep on piling up, and for the most part we keep pushing it down into a dark corner in the basement. Instead of reflecting and healing, we developed our own emotional toolkits that allowed us to survive ongoing emotional trauma.

One emotional tool my parents gave me early on was "you gotta be twice as good as white folks" to have a chance in this society. The idea, I suspect, when my parents gave me this tool was to encourage me to work hard and always do my best; never let white folks see you stumble. Many Black parents arm their children with this survival tool in order to prepare them for the harsh reality of racism and inequality in America. But tools like this also become lenses on how we see the world. The lens says that we are not as free as white people to fail, and therefore we should instead play it safe and survive because failure is much worse than surviving.[1] The lens also centers whiteness and requires that we carefully choose how we talk or dress in order to conceal our Blackness. The lens may be useful as a survival tool in a racist America, but it distances us from being able to heal from our collective trauma and restore our full humanity. Only we can do that.

Black folks are not the only ones who use lenses to see the world; we all do. We all have a tendency to analyze before we reflect. It's just easier to identify a problem or situation than it is to explore our inner vulnerability. After all, we are rewarded in our society for our ability and skill with using our lenses. When we go to work, we are handed a shiny new pair of lenses that focus our vision on solving problems, analyzing data, building partnerships, teaching, counseling, managing—all of which are external to our own reflection. When we are in school, we are socialized in ways that encourage learning by gathering information, memorizing facts, and discussing ideas that are external to our own self-reflection. In fact, researchers are now discovering the limits of "learning through our lens," or what they call cognitive learning. Schools generally focus on building students' academic skills because we assume that these skills are a good predictor of success. Reading, calculating, analyzing, and predicting are all assumed to be essential skills for both school and workplace. But researchers are now exploring "noncognitive" qualities among students and workers as potential predictors of success.

Social emotional learning has recently gained popularity among school leaders, classroom teachers, and employers. Social emotional learning focuses on the development of nonacademic skills and attributes such as self-reflection, perseverance, and integrity. These are soft skills that are not often cultivated in standardized academic curricula. While there is also considerable debate about the relative importance of noncognitive qualities for academic and workplace success, it is becoming clear that the capacity for self-reflection, introspection, and mindfulness is becoming more and more important in our lives.

In fact, researchers have found that self-reflection can cultivate better decision making, healthier relationships, and more effective leadership. Researchers at the University of Florida recruited 373 people with leadership positions in their organizations, and over a three-week period the participants were asked to reflect on and write about "three things you like about yourself that make you a good leader," "three valuable skills that you have that make you a good leader, "three useful traits that you possess that make you a good leader," "three personal achievements that you are proud of that make you a good leader," and "three things that you are good at that make you a good leader." They found that the regular practice of self-reflection—regular journaling in response to self-reflective questions—enhanced people's clarity in decision making. These people experienced greater energy and were more engaged with team problem solving.

In order to give you a deeper understanding into why this practice was so useful for these leaders, I want to lead you through a short exercise. Grab a piece of paper and a pen. Don't worry, I'll wait. Now first, I want you to free write for one minute how you are feeling in this moment about your job and the work you are doing there. Get it all out. No one else will read this but you, so you have freedom to be fully transparent.

After you have done that, notice how you are feeling in this moment. For some, your heart rate might feel accelerated and your hand might be pulsating from gripping your pen or pencil tightly as you wrote out your points of frustrations, failures, and setbacks.

Next I want you to reflect and write your response to the following two prompts: What are three things that you like about yourself that make you good at your job? And what are three personal achievements that make you proud of the work that you do?

Now read that back to yourself. Notice how you are feeling in your body. Do you feel lighter? Did you smile as you reflected back to an old note left by a student or some other moment of accolades you received?

## WHAT IS MIRROR WORK?

But how can a pivot to self-reflection support our collective healing and shifting our culture? What does a mirror have to do with social change? For more than twenty years, I've worked with community organizations around the country to enhance how they work with BIPOC young people. In most cases, my work has involved training with staff, discussions with board members, or coaching with executive directors. Most of these organizations either struggled with funding, experienced high turnover and burnout of staff, or had challenges collaborating or working with other organizations. The people I worked with are good people, with earnest commitment to supporting young people and their families. The biggest problem that I've seen, in nearly every person I've worked with, is that they simply didn't have the time, skills, or interest to reflect. There are three lessons that I've learned from my engagement with these organizations' leadership, frontline staff, and their young people.

First is that **the culture of our organizations isn't built for self-reflection**. People just don't have time in the day to sit with mindful attention to how things are going or don't take responsibility for things when they go wrong. Our days are mostly filled with to-do lists and endless tasks and meetings that push the idea of reflection to the back burner where it is seen as "something nice to do if I had the time." Take for instance your own job: How much time do you spend per week journaling your reflections about how you are contributing to the problems you are trying to solve? How often do you sit with your colleagues to discuss how folks are feeling about their work? When things don't go the way we want them to in our workplace, or in our personal lives, our tendency is to put on our lenses. When we put on lenses, we immediately place the responsibility elsewhere, and anywhere except ourselves. It's just easier to use a lens because neither our society nor our organizations are really good at using mirrors.

A couple of years ago we held a training with a collection of community organizations all serving one neighborhood. The organizations were all doing good work, but they didn't work together, didn't trust each other, and in some cases would publicly shame each other in meetings. Needless to say, there was a lot of emotional history of hurt, shame, and disappointment to wade through among the participants. We wanted to hear from everyone in the room about what they hoped would come from our meeting and how we could support the community with having vulnerable conversations. We also wanted to unearth how people were feeling about all the challenges among the organizations. Our team knew it would be a tough training, but we were committed to taking the steps to heal some of the divisions among the groups. One thing I always say to groups is that "organizations don't have problems with each other, people do." So as it turns out, some of the directors felt betrayed when they didn't get funded; others felt that some people weren't committed to the community because they weren't born there. Still others just held on to personal beefs from past interactions with people. The tension in the room was thick, and folks spoke passionately without hesitation.

One of the directors calmly stood up and said:

*I've been a part of this community for years, I was born here, raised my kids here, and I go to church here. Twenty years ago, we had a meeting like this one, where we blamed a local business for not providing us with enough funding. Ten years ago we had a community meeting about how the government needed to do more in our community. I wonder who we will be pointing the finger at twenty years from now! When are we going to hold up a mirror to ourselves and hold ourselves accountable for working better together? There is always going to be something outside our community to focus on, but we need to spend some time taking a look at ourselves first.*

It was like one of those aha moments that Oprah talks about, when someone calls out the truth in a way that's so honest that you can't help but agree. As people shared, it became clear that the history of economic exploitation in the community, combined with manipulative philanthropy, put people and organizations at odds with one another. They competed for scarce resources while attempting to solve expensive problems. Problems like violence, homelessness, and unemployment can't be solved with a four-person staff and a two-hundred-thousand-dollar budget. These factors simply made it difficult for anyone working in the community to have time, skills, or interest in reflection and taking a step back to look at the bigger picture and each person's place in it.

But taking the time for reflection isn't expensive—it's a matter of priority, not price. This leads to my second lesson working with organizations and people, which is that **using a mirror is really hard work, and it's a process, not a quick fix**. It's easy to say, "Hey, we all need to take time to do mirror work," but it's much harder to actually do it because it requires vulnerability and honesty, two things we just aren't that good at as a society. Instead, we protect and defend ourselves with armor, to use researcher and writer Brené Brown's term. For BIPOC communities, and other groups that aren't white, male, straight, and wealthy, we pick up that armor for good reason. Lord knows, I armor up every time I feel my intelligence is challenged, or when white people claim that they know Black culture better than I do. That's just being honest, folks! Brené Brown says that we often "lead from hurt" and for the most part "we work our shit out on other people, and we can never get enough of what it is we're after, because we're not addressing the real problem,"[2] which is hurt, anger, shame, and fear. But only a mirror can show us that and help us grapple with the truth.

The truth is, reflection is tough work because it requires that we all take responsibility in creating the future we want. Activist and scholar Grace Lee Boggs reminds us that social change is fundamentally about individual and collective responsibility for creating, imagining, and relating together in new ways. Mirror work, or self-reflection, is a commitment to a process and a way of seeing the world that is an interconnected whole, rather than individual cogs in a machine. I've had countless conversations with leaders in local governments, philanthropy, and civic organizations about the need to cultivate mirror work in their profession. We talk about the need to shift the values and culture of their organizations, but they approach these issues as problems to be fixed rather than a possibility to be cultivated. They say, "Yeah, that sounds nice, Shawn, but I'm just not sure where to start and what to do next because there is important work that needs to be done." Statements like this imply that mirror work and self-reflection aren't really work at all but something that might be useful if there is enough time, which of course never happens.

A few years ago, I had one of these conversations with a young and really brilliant brotha who led the Mayor of Seattle's Youth Opportunities Commission. He is tall and always impeccably dressed, and when he talks his passion to improve things for Black children in Seattle splashes over you like a warm shower. You can feel his goodness vibrate when he talks, like the bassline of a funky song. For some reason, after a speech I delivered in the city years ago, Anthony sought me out as someone he could confide in. From time to time I'll get a text from Anthony; the last one read:

> *Greetings dear Brother!*
> *I have two things I need to speak*
> *with you about . . .*

Usually when I get a text like that, it means the sender wants a letter of recommendation for a job or graduate school. But Anthony just wanted some time to sit and talk with me. No agenda, no specific outcomes, just some time to let me know what was on his mind and listen to what he had been reflecting on. He had just been appointed by the mayor to lead a small staff within the city government to focus on creating opportunities for BIPOC youth in the city. He was excited, and for the first time, the profile of this position gave him the status and stature to really make stuff happen.

But when we connected, he shared with me all the problems he was having at work and described how toxic the culture of his department had become. People were pointing fingers and blaming each other for mistakes, there was no trust or team spirit, and the leadership was out of touch with what was happening. On top of all that, he explained that the subtle racist microaggressions from his colleagues were becoming intolerable. He feared that he was becoming a "cog in the machinery" of the city government and was losing his passion for youth engagement and community involvement. Years prior to his role as director of youth and community services, he had worked in small community organizations and had established a solid reputation across the city. Anthony was trying his best to "suck it up," you know, just deal with it. But now he was at his emotional limit and was confused and really didn't know if he should suck it up and stay because it was such an important position, or if he should leave and take his talents elsewhere.

We all have experienced times like this, when things at work or at home just suck. We might feel helpless, angry, or confused, and for the most part, we put our heads down and just do our best to move through it. But moving through it or sucking it up comes with a consequence, and for Anthony it was his health. Turns out that his wife had urged him to get a checkup, and when he found the time in his full schedule to go to the doctor, his blood pressure was off the charts for his age.

When we talked, I asked him a simple question. *What do you want?* It's really a simple question when you think about it, but for a lot of us it's a really hard question to answer, mostly because we use a lens and not a mirror. When we use a lens, we might answer this question with things external to us, like more money or a better job. But the truth is, we want peace of mind and happiness. Anthony didn't appreciate the question at first, so when I asked it, his eyes tightened and he tilted his head to the side as if to say, "Haven't you been listening to me?" The question *what do you want?* requires that we hold up a mirror and reflect, ponder, explore, and wrestle with what really matters for us. The more we do this, the clearer we become. It means going inside, taking time to let the noise and chatter of the outside world settle, so that we can see with more clarity. Sometimes clarity can come in a moment, and other times it emerges slowly like a flower in a garden.

Anthony's clarity came in the moment he realized that his work was literally killing him. He and his wife spent some time wrestling with *what do you want?* A month or so later, Anthony came back with a remarkable answer to my question. "I want to be happy, healthy, and whole," he shared with me during our phone conversation. Turns out he and his wife had decided that he should leave his job and take some time off to address his medical issue. "I'm not sure how we are going to afford me leaving my job, but we're gonna figure it out . . . we are really clear about that."

Clarity was his mirror's gift. We all have access to clarity when we turn to our mirrors and trust and listen to what they say. Reflection means asking ourselves tough questions like, Am I really happy? What do I really want in life? Where is my life headed? Sometimes if we are lucky, we have friends and family who can help us wrestle with these questions, but we can also hold up our mirrors and play with these questions ourselves. From time to time, in my courses at San Francisco State University, I ask my students to reflect on these questions. Whatever the course's topic, I always integrate opportunities for my students to practice mirror work because I believe that social transformation is connected to transforming ourselves.

The third lesson that I've learned is that **social change is deeply connected to our own healing, reflection, and well-being**. I've come to realize that so much of our work to improve social conditions and solve social problems has almost entirely focused on things external to us; we just haven't learned or created opportunities for deep reflection. During my classes at San Francisco State University, I might ask my students to write a letter to their ten-year-old self. What would you say to that child? What would you want that ten-year-old child to know? What advice would you give? Next, I ask them to record a video that will be sent ten years into the future. The video is advice to yourself ten years into the future. What do you want your future self to know? What is holding you back and what are you worried about? What do you dream your life will look like in ten years? For most of my students, these activities are really hard because they require them to turn inward, and away from the safety of the textbook. Some of them struggle to understand how their own reflection on these questions is connected to the topic of a course titled "Children, Youth and Social Change." They wonder how reflecting on their own childhood will help them with their grade in my class, and why we spend so much time talking about their dreams rather than preparing for the midterm exam. But this is exactly my point, which is to use reflection as a tool for social problem solving and to create opportunities for students to turn inward. These spaces simply are rare on college campuses and are rarely cultivated in college classrooms because we all have been socialized to believe that solving social problems is about fact gathering, theorizing, analyzing, and acting, all the external stuff that privileges intellect over contemplation. So our first step is to consider the connections between deep self-reflection and social change. When we weave these two seemingly unrelated things together, we heal ourselves, our communities, and our movements.

To keep it real, I didn't always see the connection between social change and reflection and mirror work. I guess mirror work became important to me when I realized that something was really wrong in my own life. In 2001 I experienced a sort of a mental breakdown. We had just given birth to our daughter, Nyah, I was teaching at Santa Clara University, I was the executive director of a nonprofit organization in Oakland and constantly raising money, and I was leading a series of youth organizing sessions with young people. One night, I woke up in a sweat and I just couldn't sleep. I was so stressed and worried about failing to raise money, not being good enough at teaching, and most importantly not being there for my daughter. I walked into the living room and broke down crying. Well really, I was sobbing, and at first I was surprised and didn't know where all this emotion was coming from. But when I tried to calm it, bury it, and stuff it back down, it welled up even more.

I was five minutes into my snotty-nose crying when the inner dialogue started in my head. One voice, the strong baritone Black man voice, stood up and said, "Hey, you a grown-ass man, suck it up and keep it moving." Then, another voice, one that I'd really never heard before, said, "It's OK, man, you are so hard on yourself, just let go of all this shit you've been carrying," more sobbing. Nedra, my spouse, heard me and came into the living room in the midst of my emotional battle. She had never seen me in that state, so she knew something was really wrong. We just sat and talked, and what became clear to me was that I needed to make a different choice about how I wanted to live. I remember reading somewhere a quote, "I choose peace of mind, instead of this," and that's exactly how I felt.

A lot of us feel this way from time to time, and we just don't know what to do. We find ourselves on life's treadmill, and the fast pace and unlimited demands make life unbearable at times. But that's when we really need to practice reflection—it's an opportunity for us to take a break. Basically, reflection gives us an opportunity to take a look at ourselves and our lives and to assess what we really want. Reflection using our mirrors is so important in movement work as well because it allows us to take stock of what's going on inside and shatters the myth that the only real movement work happens outside of us. It also forces us to reconcile the close relationship between our inner journey and how we show up in the world on the outside.

## TRUTH, MIRRORS, AND OBSTRUCTION SPOTS

The lack of reflection in our work is the reason why we have toxic, blame-driven behavior in our movements. Leaders with the inability to reflect can work for racial justice and practice patriarchy. Advocates for justice reform who lack reflection can reinforce white supremacy, and organizers without reflection can conflate call-out culture with accountability.

I recall conducting a training for a small group of policy makers who had asked me to support their efforts to bring racial equity into their work. One of the members of the group, an older retired white man, had explained to me in our introductions that he was an expert on racial equity and had worked most of his career at bringing racial equity into large systems. He was correct; I had done my background research (à la Google) on each member of the group and learned that he had led significant racial equity efforts throughout his career, and I was impressed by his track record. He was a former trailblazing CEO of a large company where he led innovative efforts to bring racial equity into the company's policies.

The group I facilitated was multiracial, mostly women, and every time someone spoke, the older white "expert" would interrupt them by citing research as if to verify the legitimacy of what the speaker had just shared. During one exchange, a woman of color shared passionately her stress of having to always prove herself at work and how she felt insecure about talking about race in her work setting. The "expert" abruptly interrupted her, "Well . . . it is common for women from minority groups to feel uncertain. A study conducted by blah, blah, blah . . . showed that 90 percent of women from minority groups . . . blah, blah, blah." He continued, "Black and Latino women particularly have a tendency to experience racial insecurity due to the fact that they lack the confidence to lead in a corporate environment. This is why I created the first and only corporate training program for minority women to build confidence to lead in corporate environments. I'm the only person who has successfully created such a program that many companies use as a model." He continued to boast of his racial equity track record and, by the way, substantiated that her comment, and feelings about her own life experience, was in fact valid. He white-man-splained her! You know, the tendency for white men to restate, reclaim, or reaffirm that what you just said is in fact true, false, or irrelevant.

We were all in a bit of shock, but after the "expert" did this several times, I stopped him and asked if he could see that his comments could be interpreted as disrespectful and arrogant. Everyone else must have agreed with me because, one by one, people explained to him that he wasn't listening; some were insulted and angry, others expressed that they felt disrespected, and others shared how his comments created distrust. One participant explained to the "expert," "We are all speaking from our hearts here, being real with each other, and every time you speak you cut me off and talk about yourself! It's so disrespectful to me. I hope you can see what you are doing." The truth was, the "expert" simply couldn't see that his comments were racist, sexist, homophobic, and arrogant. After twenty minutes of people responding and reacting to his comments, I turned to the "expert" and asked him what was coming up for him and how he was feeling about what they said. I was intentional not to ask him what he *thought* because I wanted him to reflect more deeply on what he was *feeling* rather than rely on his research or lean on his accomplishments.

He was in his late sixties and wore a white shirt with a boring blue tie. His graying hair and beard reminded me of a professor version of Sean Connery. His animated face turned serious, and he slightly squinted his eyes as if he was attempting to solve a hard math problem. He took a deep breath, puckered his lips tightly together, and exhaled slowly, in silence. "I feel a bit embarrassed," he responded. "Umm . . . (deep inhale, exhale) let's see, I really feel some shame, and a lot of regret. This is really awkward for me, I really never intended to offend anyone, and I'm just really embarrassed and . . . I never had anyone, you know, speak to me like this . . ." *Awwww shit!* I thought to myself, *now we are getting to the nitty-gritty!*

But something miraculous had just happened to him. Maybe it happened somewhere after his lament of rescuing women of color from their own insecurity in corporate settings, and right before the poignant "sista-style" unfiltered, heated truth-telling. Or maybe it happened during the Latina sista's eloquent and graceful slicing through his white supremacy with clear passion, precision, and wisdom behind each word. It also could have happened somewhere tucked underneath the white soccer mom's meticulous explanation of how it feels to be silenced and disregarded. Somewhere in those twenty minutes, the "expert" was forced out of the comfort of his sophisticated analysis, research, data, and expertise—his lens— and gently nudged into a roomful of brand-new, polished, and perfectly working mirrors. It was the first time, it seemed, that he had come to grips with the very monster he had dedicated his career to slaying, the fragility of his own white male supremacy. When he walked into the room of mirrors, he found something remarkably unexpected—humility and vulnerability. Only a good mirror could have done that.

During the remainder of our time together, he listened with quiet curiosity about each person's story. Now, I'm not saying that he was "cured" of racism, nor was there a big Kum Ba Ya group hug at the end. But he made a pivot during our meeting, and it mattered. Something shifted inside of him, and we could tell that the honest discussion had shined a light into some hidden dark corner that he wasn't aware even existed. Sometime afterward, he commented to me, "That was the best, *worst* meeting I have ever had . . . I just thought that my experience and knowledge was helpful, but . . . well, you know, now I can see how I was showing up for people . . . and it's something I need to work on."

Maybe that is the real point of our mirror work, to reveal the truth of how we show up for others. For the "expert," he was held accountable for his comments, and the uncomfortable dialogue, truth-telling, and raw vulnerability cut through all the bullshit that sometimes fogs up our mirrors and makes things hard to see. We know what it feels like when someone speaks the truth from the heart. It burns away cloudy confusion, leaving a bright clarity in its wake. That's precisely what happened to the "expert"—he gained sight, the ability to see things that aren't easily observable. When he reflected on how his patriarchy, racism, and sexism showed up in his interactions, he could see for the first time his obstruction spots.

This can happen for us all when we cultivate the practice of reflection because it allows us to get underneath the hood and explore our motivations, fears, dreams, and insecurities with a sense of curiosity. Reflection also helps us heal some of the wounds that pile up over time in our work and personal lives that we have been refusing to take a look at. Sort of like cleaning up your house or apartment. You know damn well that you need to take out the trash, wash those dishes, throw away that pile of mail, and sweep the floor. But we find excuses not to do it, and over time the clutter builds up until we can't stand it anymore . . . you get the point. But after a good cleaning, we feel better and things seem clearer and in order.

But sometimes we don't even know we need to clean the house because we have become oblivious to the clutter; we have obstruction spots. Because we have an obstructed view, we sometimes can't see how we show up in our relationships, how we work with others, and even how we relate to ourselves. These obstruction spots are a natural by-product of our socialization, and they do a really good job of hiding things from our view. Researchers at Ohio State University's Kirwan Institute have used this idea in research on *implicit bias*, the unconscious attitudes that affect our understanding, actions, and decisions about other groups of people.[3] These researchers highlight how our obstruction spots (implicit bias) have devastating implications for ethnic groups. In the criminal justice system, obstruction spots result in a greater likelihood of conviction, longer sentences, and disproportionate incarceration among BIPOC communities. Similarly, the results can be found in education and in the practice of medicine.

In some of my own research, I have found that our obstruction spots are influenced by our social class, racial and ethnic identity, gender associations, age, and many other parts of ourselves. For example, I've found that middle-class Blacks sometimes find it difficult to understand the struggles of working-class and poor Blacks even when they are in the same family. There is an important relationship between our inner reflection about who we are and our outer action in the world. This relationship is sometimes a reflection of the harm we have experienced due to oppression and our exposure to toxic policies and practices that damage well-being. Other times this relationship is reflected in the invisible ways we are granted privilege. The truth is that no matter what our social position, this relationship (inner vs. outer) is real and connected. Our ability to reflect allows us to make this relationship more explicit in our lives and our work. When we don't reflect, our obstruction spots grow and ultimately lead to a way of seeing the world from our own perspective as the one and only truth, and we all do it. Have you ever driven a car and changed lanes without an awareness of your obstruction spot? You may have swerved into another car as it passed through your obstruction spot simply because, from your view, you concluded that the lane was clear and therefore it was OK to change lanes.

Yeah, obstruction spots are dangerous to ourselves and society—particularly when we don't even know that we have them.

## TRUE SIGHT: HINDSIGHT, FORESIGHT, AND INSIGHT

One crisp fall morning I was rushing to our office in downtown Oakland. I was about to deliver a webinar about ways that schools can better support BIPOC youth. I parked my car, got out, and headed straight for the office. There are always lots of people hanging out in front of local coffee shops or restaurants on 14th Street where our office is located. I was walking fast, with my mind on the upcoming meeting, when an elderly man suddenly grabbed my arm. "Hey, why are these young Black boys so disrespectful these days?" I was shocked, first that he actually grabbed my arm and was still holding it, and second how he knew I actually had an answer to his question and was headed to a meeting to talk about Black young men in Oakland! My parents are from the South, so I also didn't want to disrespect the elderly man and his friend that was quietly standing next to him. Both men came from that generation of Black men who worked in fields with their hands, could build an entire home with their eyes closed, and could replace a transmission in a car with a mere screwdriver. Yeah, old-school men who went into the army, returned home to raise their families with dignity and pride, and always had a cold Budweiser beer in hand. So I didn't walk away, and I listened to them both complain about Black youth and their disrespect for elders. We chatted for a while before I reached out to shake one of the men's hand as a gesture of respect before departing.

As I reached out to shake his hand, he did not reach out to shake mine. His hands rested comfortably in his pockets, and I thought to myself that perhaps he was trying to make a point about disrespect. I had assumed that he was refusing to shake my hand! His friend, the one that grabbed my arm as I was walking by, noticed the awkward interaction and said, "Aww no . . . he can't see you." I was puzzled and thought to myself, what do you mean he can't see me?

The non-hand-shaker Black man, the elder, the one from the old school, said to me, "Yeah, young man, I'm completely blind, I can't see . . . but I always know exactly where I'm at!"

How do we know exactly where we're at when sometimes it's hard to see where we've been, where we are, and where we are going? How do we shine light on our obstruction spots and gain sight from places where it's hard to see? The man who was without sight but knew exactly where he was had an answer to these questions. Despite the fact that he was physically unable to see, his ability to lean on his past, imagine a future, and reflect on the present—his mirror work—gave him another level of sight. Ruby Sales said it best in a podcast with Krista Tippett.[4] She commented that true sight, the real ability to see, involves hindsight, foresight, and insight. Together, these forms of sight provide a more complete exploration of our society and our place in it, which is after all what mirror work is all about.

## Hindsight

When we use hindsight, we often associate it with mistakes in the past, like when we say, "In hindsight, I would have never taken that job had I known what I know now." But hindsight doesn't always come from reflecting on past mistakes, though mistakes offer us great lessons; rather, *hindsight* is a culmination of lessons from key events, dilemmas, and situations in the past.

Depending on your age, you may remember with clarity and detail the events on September 11, 2001. You probably remember where you first learned about the attacks on the World Trade Center in New York. You might be able to recall the conversations you had and how you felt in the aftermath of the attacks. You might remember your teacher or principal calling everyone into the gym, or your supervisor sending everyone home that day. I vividly remember keeping my young children at home that day with our eyes glued to the TV for news updates.

Your hindsight on that event may offer you lessons about how our society might respond to a future crisis. It may also provide clarity on what really matters in life and what things are just not that important. Hindsight gives us the capacity to look back and create important lessons that propel us into better decision making, which can be used in the future. When we practice hindsight, we ask ourselves questions about key events, circumstances, and people in our past. Here are a few questions that help lean into hindsight as a tool for reflection. Reflecting on these questions means using our hindsight as a way to better understand ourselves and our power in shaping the future.

- ▶ Knowing what I know now, would I have done anything differently?

- ▶ What is the major lesson or takeaway from this situation?

- ▶ What could I have done better, or where might I have grown?

- ▶ How will this help me in the future?

- ▶ Why is this an important lesson for our society?

- ▶ What can this teach me about improving our society and humanity?

## Foresight

Hindsight of course is tethered to *foresight*, which is the capacity to imagine a possible future. Foresight pushes us to embrace the lessons from the past in order to reimagine, predict, and create what we want in our lives and in society. Foresight is not a calculated set of rules based on mathematical predictions and strategic modeling. That's not what I'm talking about. Foresight is emergent and creative while also insightful and wise. Foresight is the capacity to take key lessons from the past and combine them with a passion to create a possible future. Listen to me really closely here. Our tendency is to get locked into hindsight and never move past it. I've seen this happen in all sorts of ways with community activists, social service professionals, and corporate leaders. Traumatic and painful experiences from the past are the most enduring experiences and situations to learn from, and they are most likely to bind us to the past. We mull over the pain, discomfort, and turmoil until it determines, predicts, and becomes our future. That is why we have to learn from the past without it becoming our future. In fact, researchers have found that bad news, negative feedback, and traumatic events have a much stronger impact on our self-concept than good news, pleasant experiences, or positive feedback.[5] We just tend to recall and remember unpleasant negative experiences more than positive ones. Some researchers believe this is because humans are wired to avoid pain and negative experiences at all costs.

For instance, if I ask you to think back to what you did yesterday and recall anything that comes to mind and jot it down, if you're like me you have to think really hard about yesterday. But after a while, your strongest thoughts will gravitate toward the stressors you encountered. It might be how you woke up with a crick in your neck, or the person that nearly ran you off the road on your way to work, or how someone stole your lunch out of the public refrigerator, things like that. In order to recall good things, you need to fully focus your attention on it. It might take lots of effort to say, "Did my daughter hug me before I left for work? Wait, she sure did, and she told me that she received an A on her book report at school." Our hindsight on past trauma and negative experiences is a natural mechanism built into our survival. Yet we have to be aware of how this tendency can lock us into the past, unable to see the future or even experience the present.

True sight means that we build the muscle for this type of reflection with foresight. We build foresight when we cultivate the ability to imagine, dream, hope, all the while holding our key lessons from the past. Our brains are also built for learning from the past in order to create a possible future. Researchers identified evidence that our brains allow us to mentally travel through time.[6] There are numerous studies that examine terms such as *mental time travel, self-projection*, and *prospection*, all of which mean that our prefrontal cortex, posterior regions, and medial temporal lobes are designed for us to move between experiences from our past and projected experiences in our future. The capacity for hunter-gatherers to project where food might be a year in advance or for us to imagine our next job comes from the same place in our brains. We are literally built for foresight and our brains require that we practice imagination.

Black folks have our own term for this of course—Afrofuturism, the ability to imagine a world not bound by time and the constraints of the past, nor a predetermined future. Afrofuturism encourages permission for us to work the hell out of our prefrontal cortexes, exercise our temporal lobes so that we can boldly dream, and build an audacious imagination and have the courage to time travel without apology. More on this topic later, but for now we can begin to build our muscle for foresight in the following ways:

- Ask where my life is going, and what it will take to get me there.

- Develop a clear picture of what I really want in life, not what I settle for.

- If I could have any three things ten years from today, what would they be?

- How can my gifts contribute to a more humane and caring society?

## Insight

Insight is the elixir of deep hindsight and powerful foresight mixed together with just the right balance of each, just when we need it. Sometimes an insight can come in an instant like a brilliant idea, concept, or vision, while others take time to cook like a good gumbo! The key is that we become relentless in our mirror work, always time-traveling back to the past and leaning into the future in order to be clear in the present. Yeah, I know it's a lot easier to say this than it is to do it. Most of the time we are beating ourselves up about the past or thinking that the future is unrealistic. For me, late at night or in traffic, I turn to that TV show in my mind called "If I Woulda, Coulda, Shoulda." It's an awful show that never ends, has no commercial breaks, and is always on repeat. Each episode focuses on things I *would* have done, *could* have done, or *should* have done about a situation, interaction, or conflict. Whenever I watch it, I feel pretty beat-up afterward, so in order to feel better again I watch another episode. That's why we need to build the muscle for *insight*, which is the capacity to be present and observe the noisy chatter in our minds. Insight is like standing back and observing ourselves watch the TV show without becoming it!

Insight doesn't come from reading about it; it is cultivated through practice. Tough, hard, get-your-ass-up-and-do-it-again type of practice. Practicing insight means that we give ourselves permission to fall down, mess up, and brush ourselves off and try it again. Listen, I don't want folks to think that I'm suggesting we all go away on a silent retreat at a Buddhist monastery—though that would be an amazing way to learn and practice insight. What I am suggesting is that we've become a culture where terms like *innovation*, *strategic planning*, and *design thinking* have replaced terms like *moral compass*, *ethical decisions*, *gut feelings*, and *spirit*. This is where insight resides, and we simply can't access our insight from these highly technical quick-fix processes. Insight comes from developing the habit of sitting with uncertainty, building the inner strength to walk with calmness in the midst of a shitstorm, and leaning into the discomfort of conflict.

Insight is perhaps one of the most difficult areas of our mirror work to practice. It's difficult because insight requires that we begin to build our individual and collective capacity to observe ourselves even while in the vicious grips of racism, patriarchy, homophobia, and other forms of oppression. Insight is not a retreat from fighting racism, confronting patriarchy, and dismantling homophobia—on the contrary, it makes our efforts better and more effective.

Take for instance the legendary activist Grace Lee Boggs, who shows us through her own reflection the key ingredients to social change. Boggs, an activist and philosopher writing about the relationship between our social world and inner life, reminds us that real lasting social change requires that people

> not only struggle against existing institutions. They must make a philosophical/spiritual leap and become more "human" human beings. In order to change/transform the world, they must change/transform themselves.[7]

She is able to make this claim because of the insight she has gained from her years of really understanding people and what makes societies change. When we cultivate insight, we gain the ability to go both wide and deep, understand the past and envision the future, work on the inside and on the outside, and dance between individual change and social transformation. Insight gives us the final "third" eye to see things are not easily visible, like things that trigger us or knowledge of our vulnerabilities and strengths. Insight gives us the capacity to identify our own patterns of behavior and their connection to our collective trauma and potential for social transformation. Our individual journey and collective journeys are bound together and insight—our mirror work—helps us see this, and it shines a brilliant light on our individual and collective obstruction spots.

## CLEANING YOUR MIRRORS

When we pivot from lens to mirror, we gain the ability to move forward in our lives with confidence of sight. We all have obstruction spots that, for one reason or another, just get in the way of our ability to be clearer, better, stronger, and more present. The thing is, we can't always *see* our obstruction spots; that's because they are hidden from our view. But ask someone close to you, that you know really well, and chances are they can see things that you don't because they see you from another perspective. The only way to see through the fog of confusion, to chart a new direction, is for us to all begin our practice of using our mirrors. Here are a few suggestions to get you started on your way.

- ▶ Make the decision to practice mirror work every day by asking yourself questions like:

  - ‣ Where is my life going, and what will it take to get me there?

  - ‣ What do I really want in life? What have I been settling for?

  - ‣ If I could have any three things ten years from today, what would they be?

  - ‣ What am I learning about myself and how better to serve our society?

- ▶ Every night take inventory of what you learned about yourself; jot it down in a journal.

- ▶ Solicit feedback from people you trust and feel safe with, people who are close to you and listen without being defensive. Ask them, "If there was one thing I need to work on, what would you say it should be?"

- ▶ Tell someone close to you the three most important lessons you learned about yourself last year and how you are building on these lessons.

- ▶ Create a "mirror group," a small group of trusted friends and colleagues who can support each other in their journey for ongoing reflection.

# 2

# *Truth*

*Well . . . um . . . what had happened was . . .*

I don't remember the very first time I told a lie, but I certainly remember the last. I lied to my wife about . . . well, you know, the things husbands lie to their wives about. At first I thought nothing about the lie I told her, and I was sure her persistent inquiry, her constant, precise, detectivelike questions, her insatiable hunger for the truth would blow over and fade away if I stuck to the lie long enough. The truth is, Nedra records every subtle response in the tone of my voice, the split-second delay in responding to a question, every detail of my raised eyebrow, and the placement of my lips during her inquisitions. She files my responses away in a detailed, sophisticated, color-coded, Dewey Decimal–like filing system that would put the Library of Congress to shame. I've never seen this filing system myself though. Naw, that's top secret, and she has it locked away deep in a vault, and no matter how hard I might try to get a peek of its contents, she denies that it even exists. I know it's there though, because sometimes I bend the truth about something minor or irrelevant (at least to me) only to have that "bent truth" show up as Exhibit A in a well-crafted argument years later. From time to time, she will drop on me verification, with solid documentation, that I'm lying by retrieving hard evidence from her vault. She will show conflicting facts that don't fit neatly together, highlight my inconsistencies with laser-like logic, and conclude in her closing argument that "either you lied to me in 2015, Shawn, or you are lying right now . . . which is it?" In times like this, when her evidence is just too damn clear, when her superior file keeping is without blemish, when I'm overwhelmed by her logic and reason, I'm left with only one thing to say, "Well . . . um . . . what had happened was . . ."

Searching for the truth is not only a personal endeavor; some of us are paid to search out, hunt down, and discover the truth. Detectives are hired to find evidence of the truth when it's hidden, doctors search for the truth about the causes of our illness, journalists investigate and swim through facts in order to uncover the truth about matters. Though the rest of us may not make a living out of it, we seek the truth in our personal lives through the relationships we have with our children, family members, coworkers, and other folks with whom we associate. If we are lucky, we have people around us who can thrust a mirror into our face from time to time, in order to cajole, elbow, or shove us into the realm of truth-telling.

In our movements and efforts to create a just and equitable society, our obstruction spots sometimes get in the way of our ability for truth-telling. I learned this lesson years ago when I attended college at San Diego State University. I had secured a great job working with high school students over the summer. One of my mentors at the time had started this summer program with her own money and had garnered some financial support from other organizations like the San Diego Urban League, NAACP, and several Black sororities and fraternities. We discussed my modest pay for the six-week summer program, which I gladly accepted. It was an amazing summer spent mentoring and teaching Black youth the ins and outs of college life, taking them camping, and coordinating a host of other activities.

It wasn't until two weeks into the program that I noticed that I hadn't received my paycheck. My rent was due, student loan was long gone, and I had counted on this job to get me through the summer. After I approached my mentor about not receiving my paycheck, she told me to expect the check next week. Next week turned into a month, and a month turned into, well, you get it. I never was paid, and she never told me the truth. Turns out she didn't raise the money she needed and had hired me and a few of my friends to run the program with hopes of securing our pay—but that never happened. Rather than sitting us down and telling us the hard truth about what was going on, she simply brushed it under the rug and led us to believe our paychecks were on the way. I've let it go, but I was hurt, disappointed, and angry because after six weeks of leading icebreakers, dropping kids off at home, breaking up fights, conducting workshops, making sandwiches, renting equipment, and calling parents, my landlord was evicting me! The truth would have helped me make the decision to either find another job altogether or stay knowing I would not be paid.

Life has an ironic way of teaching lessons. Twenty years after my "all work no pay" deception, I found myself in the same seat as my mentor. Me and a group of friends had built a successful nonprofit organization in Oakland, California, called Leadership Excellence. For nearly twenty years, we had worked with African American youth and secured critical funding from the City of Oakland for our summer programming. I had transitioned to the board of directors and wasn't involved in the day-to-day activities when I learned that our executive director was on vacation in Puerto Rico at a crucial time before the summer programs were to begin. We had hired our entire summer staff (approximately thirty college-age counselors) to work in our programs. I can't remember how I learned that our funding from the City of Oakland had not been entirely secured. You see, in order to receive our funding, we needed to submit stacks of paperwork, multiple forms with signatures, and provide proof of this and that. I had assumed that all the paperwork for our funding had been completed before the executive director left on vacation and that everything was on track and running smoothly as it always had been! Things were far from smooth because the paperwork had not been completed and therefore our funding was not coming. We had hired a group of excited, dedicated, committed counselors, without the money to pay them! It would be months before we had the cash we needed to make the payroll over the summer.

OK, so what do you do when you know there is a payroll of thirty people you can't pay?

A. You can stall and tell them everything is fine, and there will be a slight delay in receiving paychecks.

B. Lie, tell them there is nothing wrong, and pretend that things will work themselves out.

C. Tell them the god's honest truth, the money isn't available, and you don't know when they will be paid.

Truth is, I wanted to select B because I just didn't have the courage, time, or energy to tell them the truth. I actually began with A at first; then I remembered back to how I felt twenty years ago when I was in their shoes. I remembered how angry I felt for being taken advantage of, and the sinking gut feeling I had when my landlord taped an eviction notice to my door.

It had taken me a few days to come to grips with what I needed to tell them. Rumors had begun to spread, and folks were calling and texting me for answers. So I requested a meeting on a Friday afternoon in July at one of the youth centers. The large meeting room served as both cafeteria and auditorium, and I could still smell hints of the lunch they had served hours before. Many of the counselors I had known from my work in the community, and up until now we had great relationships. But now, just about everyone in the room, all thirty of them, had the "you messing with my money" look on their faces, and there weren't any pleasant greetings, fist bumps, or what ups. It was about to go down, and I was going to tell them the truth.

## VERITAS, GODDESS OF TRUTH

So what is truth anyway, and why is it important? The concept of "something that is true" was first recorded in the mid-fourteenth century and referred to as a state of being open, not hidden, having fidelity and authenticity. The term is derived from Old English *tréwp* and has been contemplated by the Greeks, Romans, Zulu, Aztecs, and Mayans. *Veritas*, in Roman mythology, is the goddess of truth, and the term can be found in *"Veritas vos liberabit,"* "The Truth Will Set You Free," embedded in university mottos because it conveys a sense of loyalty to knowledge and pursuit of uncovering what is hidden.

For the most part, truth as a concept was studied in the realms of philosophy and religion. The French philosopher Michel Foucault, for example, examined the concept of truth and its relationship to power. He explored how truth, or the lack of truth, reinforced basic assumptions about how our society functions. He promoted the idea that the concept of truth is based on what we collectively assume to be true, which often binds societies to invisible rules that control and subjugate. Foucault was a postmodern philosopher who rejected the idea that there were absolute truths; rather he thought about the ways that truth is defined by our race, culture, gender, social class, physical ability, sexual orientation, and so on. Truth, according to Foucault, is relative, contextually defined, and not easily verified from evidence or proof.

In several of his books, Foucault uses the term *parrhesia* (yeah, I know, that's hard for me to pronounce too . . .), which translates to English as "free speech." Someone who is said to use parrhesia is someone who speaks their mind, shares what's on their heart, talks with complete honesty, and communicates without fear. The word *parrhesia* also conveys a relationship between the one who speaks and the one who receives "the honest" truth. Generally, when this occurs, according to Foucault, we can "feel" the truth because when it is spoken from the heart, the truth pierces through us and resonates deep inside. This is at the heart of Nedra's filing system— she can "feel" the truth when it comes from the soul. Parrhesia goes beyond the conventional notion of free speech, the idea that members of a society have the freedom to express their views without punishment. The term also highlights the sense of freedom we experience when we speak from the soul and express ourselves through our spirit. When we speak in this way, this form of truth-telling is emancipatory, frees us from the weight of deception, and lifts the heavy burden of carrying the lie. "Ye shall know the truth, and the truth shall make you free" (John 8:32).

This concept, parrhesia, is not unique to French philosophy nor European social theory. Walk into any Black church on a Sunday morning and you'll see it right after the choir sings, and right before the praise offering; we call it *testifying*. The Black gospel tradition is rooted in a form of truth-telling that heals the scars of racial oppression and soothes the souls of the rejected. Testifying, like parrhesia, is based on telling the truth from the soul without the worry of consequences. Testifying in the Black church involves the act of publicly praising God's role in getting people through "troubled waters" in life. To testify in the Black church is akin to a truth-telling ritual that is both intensely personal and magnificently public. The dance between the two, a personal story of overcoming trauma and "troubled waters" and witnessing the story together, forms an elixir of healing for both the teller and the listener.

Similarly, the term *testimonio* in the Latinx tradition is understood as "witness account," or a firsthand story, of political or social injustice. Testimonio was created by Chicana/o scholars who sought to depart from conventional methodological traditions where objectivity and secondhand evidence were taken at face value. Testimonios are driven by a form of truth-telling about events, experiences, and issues that are often silenced, hidden, denied, and covered up by the powerful elite. Telling the story of what happened is both political, because it provides a counternarrative about injustice or oppression, and personal, because sharing the story empowers, heals, and validates the storyteller. Again we see here the relationship between truth, liberation, and freedom, "the truth shall set you free."

Truth-telling is also a cornerstone of many Indigenous nations. The concept of truth-telling is based on the idea that stories about the history and future hold sacred knowledge. Through these stories, families and communities govern, lead, and live with the responsibility to tell the truth about Indigenous histories. One such concept, "haa-huu-pah," is a form of truth-telling that demonstrates how

North American Indigenous stories are vital sources of resilience and are critical to the resurgence of Indigenous communities.

In 1955 Mamie Till didn't use the term *testimonio* when she insisted on an open-casket funeral on the South Side of Chicago. She wanted to tell the truth so the world could see the horrors of how racism could mutilate, break, puncture, and deform her beautiful brown fourteen-year-old son's body. It was perhaps her truth-telling that sparked the movement for civil rights in America. In 2012 Sybrina Fulton, Trayvon Martin's mother, didn't call her truth-telling *testifying* when she called attention to her son's murder at the hands of George Zimmerman. In 2014 Samaria Rice never used the word *parrhesia* when she told the truth about her beautiful twelve-year-old boy Tamir, who was fatally shot by a Cleveland police officer for playing with a pellet gun in a nearby park. Their truth-telling, along with the voices of too many Black mothers and fathers who have lost their sons and daughters to sanctioned murder, helped launch the movements for Black lives, perhaps the most significant truth-telling movements of our time.

Despite how we used the term *truth* (truth and reconciliation, speaking truth to power, true north, ground-truthing), it all boils down to one thing: having clarity about our story and sharing it. Scores of social scientists have attempted to measure, predict, examine, and test just about every variation of the concept of truth you can think about. Researchers at the University of California, San Diego, Emotion Lab wanted to know if compassion influences our level of truth-telling. They learned that if you care about someone, you are more likely to be honest with them.[1] But research also shows us that speaking truth to power is good for our health. Researchers at the University of Notre Dame claim that when people managed to speak up and tell the truth or reduce their lies during a ten-week study, they reported significantly improved physical and mental health in those same weeks.[2]

More important than university research and laboratory studies about truth is the fact that honesty to ourselves and others is humanizing. When we tell ourselves the truth, we become vulnerable, honest, and transparent. Truth-telling requires that we conjure up the courage to convey what is real for us, and when we do that, we are more authentic and powerful. Sometimes, of course, we just don't know what is true for us, and what we want isn't that clear. Usually that's because we think that the truth resides in our ability to "think" our way to honesty, or we rationalize things so that the truth becomes evident. Take for instance weighing the pros and the cons about a situation in order to determine what path to take. We do this because we believe comparing, analyzing, sorting, and compartmentalizing facts can somehow reveal to us the truth. But we also experience that little voice inside, or that gut feeling deep down, that we know is guiding us. So often we don't take the time to listen to that little voice or gut feeling and discount it as something irrelevant. But that is where the truth usually resides, deep inside, tucked away beneath all the chatter. That's why it's important that we take time to just reflect on how we feel about things in our gut, or spirit, because this type of wisdom guides us to truth when we are quiet and settled enough to listen.

So what does truth-telling have to do with mirror work? And why does it matter for us individually and for our society? Truth-telling is the practice of testifying to yourself and others about what is real and honest from your perspective of the world. Over time, this process builds integrity, the opposite of bullshit, and keeps us emotionally honest about what really matters. One of the fundamental gifts of mirror work is strengthening our tools to work through the bullshit in our lives that gets in the way of honesty and dilutes integrity. This type of mirror work is hard because it's scary, painful, and messy to be honest with ourselves and others. We also don't really learn how to practice truth-telling, and so for the most part we avoid it like vomit on a park bench.

The only way to lean into our truth-telling is to do it! I know, it's scary as hell, but the first place we can start is by telling ourselves the truth.

Just start with this question: "What is the truth about myself that I've been avoiding?"

Pondering this question gets the ball rolling on our ability to practice truth-telling with ourselves. Again, it's not a silver-bullet solution as much as it is a tool for practice. We all have areas of our lives where we just don't have the right tools to deal with them, so we don't. But over time, our inability to embrace or face the truth begins to wear down and blemish our integrity. So instead of being honest with ourselves, we suck it up, grind through, and bullnose our way through life. I'm not saying that perseverance is wrong, but the problem is that sometimes perseverance is the only tool we use, and therefore we never pick up new tools to deal with life's problems.

When you think about it, we all should be able to respond to this question. Some of us don't want to admit that we are unhappy in our relationships, feel unfulfilled in our jobs, are exhausted with balancing work, school, and family, fear that we haven't achieved our dreams, avoid risk for fear of failure, or are lonely even when we aren't alone. It doesn't matter what truth you've been avoiding. The important thing is to look at it—and claim it. This is real mirror work, and yes, it's hard and messy, but when we claim our truth, we begin to heal the scars that made us afraid to tell ourselves the truth in the first place.

So much of our efforts for social change have been outward looking. We have focused on changing systems, laws, and policies in our society that create inequality and suffering. External work is necessary but still insufficient because we also need a process of healing our inner world that has been damaged, harmed, and injured by social inequality. Social transformation is also an inside job, and there is a relationship between our individual healing and social transformation, and the two cannot be separated. When we practice truth-telling, honesty, parrhesia, we slowly begin to weave a new and brilliant fabric of social possibilities.

\* \* \*

They all sat in the blue plastic chairs, all thirty of them. Fridays during our summer program are usually celebratory. After working field trips, parent calls, and a full day of activities with energetic young people all week, all the counselors are ready for a break for the weekend. But this Friday, the day I was about to tell the truth, made the air in the cafeteria real tense. After everyone settled in, I took a deep breath and began. "Thanks, everyone, for coming. I know that you're ready for your hard-earned weekend. The purpose of this meeting is to explain to you what is happening with your paychecks and I'll do my best to answer any questions you might have." OK, I'm doing fine, and even though my heart is pounding out of my chest, I'm not sure they could tell I was nervous. "I know there's been rumors about the status of your paychecks and some confusion about when you will be paid. I want to clear up a few things," I explained with trepidation.

I wanted to say to them, "Well . . . um . . . what had happened was . . ." but that phrase, those simple words, initiate a sequence of explaining adjacent truths. Not really a lie, but not really the truth either. That phrase makes it easy to bob and weave between the hard-direct jab of truth. So I said to them, "The truth is I don't know if or when you will be paid for all your hard work this summer. There were several mistakes that were made, and a few delays in applying for the funding, that I and others should have been on top of, but we weren't. These mistakes have delayed our funding source, and we are working to resolve all the issues that are preventing you from getting your check. I understand completely if you will need to quit so that you can find a paying job this summer, that is understandable." Inhale . . . and exhale . . . OK, that was the truth, at least so I thought.

## THE HARDEST LOOK IS INWARD

We generally hold two perspectives about truth-telling. The first perspective is what we call "absolute" truth, those things that hold true over time, under any situation or circumstance. Absolute truth is like the law of gravity—no matter where we go, or when we go there, the law works no matter what. This perspective views truth as something that can be obtained through objective, rational thinking. An absolute truth might be *space and time exist*, or *God is real*. These statements presume that we live in a "knowable" world where we can search for and discover what is true. The second perspective is what we call "relative" truth, which basically means that there is no absolute truth. Relative truth means that knowledge is subjective and "relative" to context, culture, values, worldview, religion, gender, and so on. What we assume to be truth is nothing more than social assumptions that influence how we see the world. The second perspective rejects the idea that there are any absolutes; everything is interpreted and filtered through our subjective experiences.

Absolute truth is like a destination, some clearly defined and universal conclusion, whereas relative truth is like the journey, meandering, discovering, pondering, and never certain that you have arrived. Both perspectives are debated in theology and the social sciences, and both assume that truth requires something outside of yourself. Truth-telling is hard because it requires us to look inward, and not only at the outside world. Neither absolute nor relative truth takes us on the inward journey that helps us reflect on things that aren't easily seen but are perhaps deeply felt.

I've worked with hundreds of teachers, social workers, and social justice movement leaders, and this idea is one that is often the hardest to practice. We live in an era when the term *fake news* has been used to discredit and call into question journalistic accounts of corporate greed, government corruption, and civil rights violations. How might truth-telling by looking inward address the atrocities we see in the world? Isn't it my responsibility to tell the truth about what is going on in the world and speak truth to power? I also hear similar concerns among my graduate students when I teach about social transformation and healing. But the thing is, we don't need to choose between outward truth-telling and inward truth-telling because these two seemingly separate forms of truth are actually the same. There is no objective nor relative truth but rather a cosmic and funky dance between both. Truth emerges in our ability to dance, sway, and pivot between both without missing the downbeat. This dance is awkward at first because we live, work, and play in a binary world defined as this or that, us and them, Black and white, good and bad. The between, the gray area, is harder to deal with, so instead we choose sides.

In music they call it the "and" in the space between 1 and 2 of the downbeat: 1 *and* 2 *and* 3 *and* 4. When we can dance in the "and," we are dancing in truth. But this takes practice, commitment, and grace. When I teach and train folks about inward and outward truth-telling, I tell a story about a couple salsa dancing. My intellectual comrade and friend Julio and I were teaching at the University of Puerto Rico at Cayey during the summer, and one evening we decided to have dinner and check out the bars in Viejo San Juan. We stopped by the Nuyorican Café, a well-known venue for poetry, music, and generally good vibes. The place was packed with folks surrounding the dance floor where a couple was performing the most eloquent, rhythmic, and, well, funky salsa I had ever seen. The guy was smooth and didn't move much but kept perfect time with his hands and eyes. The woman swayed, dipped, and swirled without missing a beat as if they were talking about the intricate detail of each step, strategically planning their next acrobatic move. He would pull her close then push her away while still gently holding her hand, and somehow, magically, they were gliding in between the rhythm, not on the downbeat, not on the 1 nor the 2, but on the *and*.

I think this is where truth is, in our ability to dance between our inward journey and our outward reality. This doesn't mean that we have to sacrifice our values of justice, fairness, and peace. Suffering is not relative, violence is not subjective, dehumanization is not contextual; they are real and have consequences for humanity. It means that in order for our movements to be transformational, we have to cultivate a way to deepen and broaden our truth-telling. Truth-telling is the practice of consistent and transparent integrity. This is why truth-telling lives in both our soul-searching introspection and keen social analysis; both are necessary.

Truth-telling in our movements, our work, and our relationships is interwoven between the personal and the public, the self and society. We cannot separate these, and our inner truth-telling (or lack thereof) is inextricability connected to our social truth-telling. This is the premise behind truth commissions, which attempt to uncover the truth by creating a container for the personal account of one's personal experience of injustice and suffering. Truth-telling is maybe one of the most significant practices in transformative movements because the process is both personal and political, individual and collective.

* * *

I wasn't concerned with objective truth or relative truth when I told those thirty young counselors that they wouldn't be paid. I didn't care about truth commissions, nor terms like parrhesia when I sat in that hot cafeteria with all eyes on me. What I had thought was the truth really just scratched the surface, and I wish I would have practiced some self-truth-telling before calling that meeting. "Does anyone have any questions?" I asked, bracing myself for fury, disdain, and righteous anger at both the message and messenger. I thought I was prepared until I got the first question.

"So, Shawn, what is your responsibility in this situation?" At first I thought the person who asked me simply hadn't heard my clear, concise, and accurate explanation of what had occurred. They must have not heard me say, "I don't know if or when you will be paid for all your hard work this summer."

So I repeated this mantra, "I don't know if or when you will be paid for all your hard work this summer," and the twenty-something-year-old counselor corrected me.

"My question wasn't when will we be paid, my question was what is *your* responsibility in this situation."

I replied, "Oh OK, um well let's see, um I've, well . . . um there are, the reality is um ahh . . ." I was ferociously stumbling, helplessly tripping, foolishly tumbling over each word, and I had abandoned my composed and precise explanation. This question was about a deeper truth, one I had not considered nor contemplated. The question wasn't about what happened but my role in it, and I wasn't ready for that question, and they knew it.

But sometimes truth-telling makes you lighter because you set down the heavy lie to be dealt with. My truth was that I didn't make it a priority to make sure they were paid. The truth was that I didn't want to get involved with all the details and bureaucratic paperwork that was required by the city. The truth was I was tired, exhausted with overseeing, managing, and problem solving. Ultimately, the truth was that I was asleep at the wheel and could have done much more to ensure they were paid. So when I told them that I was asleep at the wheel and named a few things that I could have done, I probably felt better about telling them than they did.

About two weeks later all the counselors received their checks. Our board of directors had taken out a loan so that everyone could be paid. I was relieved when the loan finally came through because I knew how it felt to work without being paid. From time to time, I still run into one of those counselors, and I'm not sure if they would tell this story the same way. They might have a completely different version of what happened. All I know is that, in our efforts to build movements based on justice, we harm each other, we lie to each other, and we make mistakes. Mirror work alone won't solve all the problems of the world, but truth-telling is a way to lean into deeper mirror work for ourselves and others. When we practice working with our mirrors, we build stronger tools for our own reflection and more durable forms of social change. As I said before, social change is an inside job. So how do you begin truth-telling, what does it look like in your relationships, and how might it show up at work? Here are a few tools that can get you started in your truth-telling process.

## ARCHITECTURE OF TRUTH-TELLING

We are actually all born knowing how to tell the truth; it's lying that we've learned how to do. But there are some things we can do to pivot back to our truthful selves and restore a sense of wholeness in our efforts for social change. In my own work, I've seen the power of truth-telling among youth workers, teachers, social workers, community organizers, and CEOs in corporate boardrooms. There seems to be a common design, or architecture, of truth-telling that I've seen over the years that when put to action pulls groups closer together, reveals social injustice, and heals personal pain. This architecture is not a magic bullet with superpowers but rather simple steps that remind us of the power of how to be human with each other.

## Tell Your Truth Story

Have you ever started planning something only to be derailed by something you didn't anticipate? Maybe someone's personality in the group is a distraction, or perhaps someone takes up too much space in phone calls or planning meetings. I've seen so many groups of well-meaning people gather for a worthy purpose only to find themselves lost after a few meetings. Typically, someone in the group has a clear agenda about why they have chosen to participate. But this agenda is not evident to everyone because there's been no intentional truth-telling process. When there isn't a clear truth-telling process, everyone has to assume or guess the motivation and intention for everyone's participation. We do this unintentionally, and it causes problems in how we show up and work together.

In just about every journey I've led, we start with an opportunity for each person to tell their story. For example, I was a board member with a diverse group of people who had committed to using racial equity as a guiding principle in the organization. However, the board had never really had an explicit conversation about race; it was largely a theoretical and conceptual exercise for most of them. This presented a potential problem because I knew that at some point in our journey we would need to have some difficult conversations about race, equity, power, whiteness, patriarchy, and so on. Rather than launch into a discussion about race or invite the experts to tell us how to lead with racial equity, we did the opposite. We started with our own stories. During one of our meetings, we rearranged the room so that all twenty chairs were in a circle, and we removed all the boardroom tables. Prior to the meeting, we had asked each board member to bring an object to the meeting that best represented their ethnic or racial journey. People brought pictures of their grandparents, secret family recipes, pictures of places, watches, newspaper clippings, and precious, delicate objects that held powerful meaning. Each person began by explaining why they chose the object and what meaning it held for them.

It's amazing what you can learn about someone when you give them the space to tell their story from a place of truth. We heard about the horrors of racial violence growing up in the South. Some shared stories about being white, adopted, and feeling like they never fit in. Others shared personal stories about being abused as a child. It was real, honest, hard to ignore, gut-bucket truth-telling, and it made all the difference in the world. When a person shares their story with someone, it creates a sacred bond between the teller and the listener. When groups invest in the time for everyone to share their story, the bond serves as a type of group-dynamics insurance policy. Shit happens, and there is going to be some tough work and hard conversations that every group encounters. The bond created by sharing each person's story, however, provides the group with a deeper layer of protection from falling apart because there is understanding and clarity about motivations shared among everyone.

## Practice Vulnerability

Most of the time, the thing that stands in the way of our truth-telling is the fear of being hurt, harmed, or rejected. It's natural to protect ourselves and those we care about from something that could be harmful. That's how we learned to bend the truth to ourselves and to others. But we also have to ask ourselves: What is the cost of leaving your personal life at the door when you go to work? How does it feel when you can't be your whole self when you work with others? Chances are that you've wrestled with the false separation between the personal and professional. Practicing vulnerability just means that we feel safe enough to say what we feel. But vulnerability also involves courage to say (or listen to) what's unpopular, uncomfortable, and sometimes even unsafe. Folks of color, LGBTQ communities, and differently abled people know what it means to be vulnerable and courageous enough to say what might be unpopular.

Practicing vulnerability also means that we use terms like *I'm curious*, *I'm feeling confused*, *I'm feeling angry*, or *I'm afraid*. Vulnerability is an important gut check because it forces us to go inward first (the hardest look is inward) and get clear about what's going on for us. Brené Brown has written extensively on vulnerability, and she says that vulnerability is perhaps the most powerful practice of wrestling with what is uncertain with emotional exposure. Practicing vulnerability is key to our mirror work and truth-telling.

## Ask about Avoided Truth

From time to time, I ask myself what truth I've been avoiding when I'm uncertain or afraid of something. Take the time when I was offered a job in New York City working for a foundation. I wasn't excited about the job, and there was something underneath my lack of motivation. Turns out my lack of motivation was fueled by raw unfiltered fear. I had convinced myself that moving my family to New York was not worth the risk, but that wasn't the real truth. When I asked myself, "What is the truth I've been avoiding?" the question made me reflect at a deeper level. Here is what I discovered:

- ► I was afraid that I might fail.

- ► I feared that I wasn't good enough for the job.

- ► I feared that I might get laid off or fired without a backup plan.

- ► I feared that my wife would be disappointed in me.

Sometimes simple questions can be powerful tools to self-discovery, one of the key ingredients to transformative social change. We have to invest time in knowing, discovering, exploring the inside journey as we also move to change our world.

*The Four Pivots*

Mirrors are silver and exact—they don't hide the truth, and they reflect back precisely what stands before them. Truth-telling is a tool and a guide that can give us more power in our work to transform our world. It's time that we move our work and ourselves to another level of awareness and engagement. No one said that mirror work would be easy, without challenge or difficulty, but isn't that the case for everything that is worthwhile?

piled up into a mound of blended chrome, black smoke, and metal. Akil was injured but OK, confused but alive. He wondered what had just happened and what had obscured his, and everyone's, visibility that day.

## SUSPENSION, SALTATION, AND CREEP

The ingredients of a dust storm are simple. It just requires dry air, sustained wind, and expansive land with soil. Dust storms are not unique to California's Central Valley; they happen all around the world. The size and scope of a dust storm depend on the quality and fineness of each dust particle. Most of the time, the particles on the surface of a field are held in place by their own weight. When the wind picks up, these particles are launched from their holding place and into the airflow of wind. When the particles are projected back onto the surface, they crash into resting particles, ejecting even more particles into the airflow, thus creating a chain reaction. Once these particles are in motion, they travel by one of three modes: suspension, saltation, and creep.

This is where it gets interesting. *Suspension* involves transport of only the finest dust particles, where airflow moves billions of them in a swirling unison. These fine dust particles may be transported to altitudes of up to 4 miles and distances of up to 3,000 miles. Usually red-colored and alkalized, these particles are suspended high in the atmosphere and contribute to the loss of visibility and make it hard to see. Movement by *saltation* is different and involves only the larger dust particles that are too heavy to travel by suspension. These are the particles that get caught in your eyes or clothing because they travel close to the ground. The last is *creep*, which moves the largest and heaviest particles that cannot be ejected from the soil so are rolled by the wind, bumping into and waking up other particles to join the traveling party. When suspension, saltation, and creep come together, mixing, swirling, laughing, dancing, and nodding their heads to the beat of "Groove Me," bad things can happen.

Around 3:00 P.M. Akil and all the travelers on I-5 met up with suspension, saltation, and creep. These devious dust particles didn't care about the children in the back seat nor the hot dinner that awaited each traveler on their long journey home. Suspension, saltation, and creep just wanted to play their mischievous and deadly game of obscuring clarity from each innocent traveler, and they played their game well on 100 miles of I-5 that day.

The travelers knew where they were headed, and I'm sure they had mapped out the journey with a sense of certainty about their destination. But suspension, saltation, and creep acted suddenly, without warning, and wrapped the travelers' world with ambiguity and covered them with confusion. We are all like those travelers on I-5, when we begin our journey toward justice only to run into swirling particles that we had not anticipated. When that happens—and it always does—we lose clarity, which is the only thing that can get us to where we want to go.

## LUCID CERTAINTY

I've seen many BIPOC leaders struggle with clouds of confusion, distraction, and ambiguity—those swirling dust particles. When we are unclear and vague, we simply cannot practice transformative leadership because we can lose sight of our destination. In some cases, I've seen leaders get so absorbed in their work that they lose a piece of themselves and obscure the reason behind their work. I've also seen leaders who have become so enmeshed in their jobs that they never could imagine doing anything else with their lives; they have become their occupation. Now, that's not to say that there is something wrong with being passionate, deeply engaged, and immersed in a desire to change things for communities. In fact, that type of commitment is required of a transformative social justice leader. But without mirror work and ongoing deep reflection, passion can slip into tunnel vision that causes us to lose sight of the bigger picture. I've seen leaders of color "hide behind" their work, choosing to solve problems at work, like making payroll, raising money, or hiring the right team, but their home life was a wreck and their personal relationships and health were in shambles.

When we practice mirror work, an ongoing commitment for self-reflection, and truth-telling, we arrive at clarity. *Clarity* can be defined as a state of vivid and transparent certainty, which illuminates an unambiguous path toward a desired goal or direction. Clarity is the ability to be lucid with a coherent awareness about your journey. There is an important distinction, though, between being clear and clarity. Being clear is about how others experience you, and it is external to your own self-awareness. Being clear might involve speaking with precision in your word choice or a well-articulated statement. Being clear is just good communication. Clarity, on the other hand, is something we feel from deep inside and involves accepting a sense of calm certainty of what is important and what is not. Being clear can come from thinking, but clarity comes from surviving a game with suspension, saltation, and creep, a dust storm, when something unexpected happens that disorients, confuses, and obscures. When we find ourselves in life's dust storms, clarity is being able to hold an unobscured vision of what is happening and take the steps you need to get through it. Clarity burns away all the opaque bullshit, leaving in its wake a lucid simplicity. Clarity comes when we shed all the barriers, confusion, distractions, amusements, and excuses that get in the way of what we really want. When you know what you want so bad that nothing can convince you otherwise, that's when you have clarity. But clarity doesn't always come to us like a lightning bolt out the sky; sometimes it's subtler and comes over time like when you realize that it's time to leave a relationship or find a new job.

My first moment of clarity came when I was called a nigger for the first time. As I write this, it's hard to imagine that my first reckoning with being called nigger wasn't until I was in high school. It happened during a high school football practice. It was hella hot and muggy that day, and we had just finished our practice and were taking a water break. We were all hot, thirsty, and tired and rushed to orange Gatorade buckets on the sideline. I stepped in front of Eric, the team captain, who was tall, arrogant, and a 250-pound white boy. He was a senior, the coaches' favorite player, and all the teachers' best student; everyone liked him. I was a skinny tenth grader, insecure and trying to fit in. My parents had moved our family from the working-class, Black side of town to a more affluent middle-class part of town people called Canyon Crest, which was mostly white. My mom explained when we moved that she wanted us to go to a better school, which also meant the schools were mostly white and affluent.

I must have forgotten that I was in hostile territory because I was surprised when I heard him calmly say to me, "Move back, nigger."

Now most of the time, being called nigger is grounds for a full assault, a go-ballistic ass whooping. It's the one time that yo mamma would pat you on the back after having to leave work early to pick you up from school because you just got suspended for fighting. Naw, fighting for being called nigger is expected, and truth be told, required. So I paused, turned slowly toward him, and replied, "What the fuck did you say?"

He replied with more emphasis, certainty, and without hesitation, "I said, 'move back, nigger.'" Everyone heard him and just chuckled and laughed as they walked by. He pushed past me and kept moving as if nothing had happened. But I was furious, not because he had called me a nigger, but because I didn't say or do anything in response. I hated myself for not swinging on him, or cussing him out, or going completely ballistic on his ass. I just stood there, holding my helmet with an embarrassing grimace on my face. I didn't say or do anything, just watched those white boys chuckle at me and let that tall white boy push me aside. I was so humiliated and disappointed in myself for being paralyzed with fear and not having the courage to stand up against him. I told myself that I would never in my life let that happen to me or anyone else again—period. That was my first moment of clarity, a lucid certainty that comes from the soul.

So why is clarity important for our work toward social justice? What are the things in our lives that get in the way of clarity? How do we cultivate clarity in our lives and in our work to improve our society? I didn't really anticipate writing about clarity because, well, most of the time, if I have to be totally honest, I don't have much clarity. I delay important decisions, procrastinate on tasks, and at times postpone key assignments mostly because I'm not clear or confident about what I'm doing. So my coping mechanism is to just put things off until clarity comes knocking on my door.

Most of the time when we study clarity as a concept, we think about it as some mystical state of mind that you get when you remove all the chatter, self-talk, and noise in your head. Clarity is also sometimes considered a goal, the cereal-box prize that you get when you go away on a silent retreat. Whenever I hear people talk about clarity, it's a revered mental state that people wish they had but don't know how to get. I suppose that's why much of the research about clarity involves asking participants to practice mindfulness as a way to build awareness of their brain chatter. Clarity of thought, in most of the research, comes from slowing down your thinking and settling into an awareness of what's in your head. I can see a brain researcher studying clarity by connecting electrodes to people's shaved heads so she can see clarity in between their brain waves. I'm not discounting the fact that mindful nonjudgmental awareness can bring clarity of thought. But I'm not talking about that type of clarity. Nonjudgmental awareness of racism, oppression, bigotry, and sexism can be dangerous. I'm talking about a clarity that comes from a purpose, conviction, and focus all rooted in justice. It's the type of clarity that comes from seeing with your eyes and your heart, outward observation and inward reflection at the same time—lens and mirror. A clarity that is felt deep down in your bones and cuts through any confusing chatter, doubt, or worry. We've all had these types of clarity, but most of the time we experience them as moments of lucid certainty. Chances are, these were powerfully lucid events that changed something significant in our lives.

Clarity is important for our collective work as social justice leaders. Sometimes in our work for justice in our movements, we get lost and confused about what really matters in efforts to heal ourselves and our society. I've seen leaders lose clarity in three ways. First, in some cases ego gets in the way, and when it does it's hard to get a handle on it. Ego is really just a way of hiding from something about yourself that you think no one can see. It's a way of protecting something that is missing, harmed, or just never nurtured or cared for. When I see ego among leaders of color, I immediately begin to think about what they might be hiding from, who hurt them, and how they never healed. It's hard to do this all the time because sometimes people are just assholes and I want to leave it at that. But that's just my ego talking, and I remind myself of the phrase "hurt people, hurt people."

But I think, for those of us who consider ourselves healers and try to move through the world with grace and compassion, we have to get under the hood a bit about why sometimes leaders, particularly leaders of color, lead with ego. What do you think happens to people when, against all odds, they seem to have overcome all the bullshit life has to throw at them? They've been hurt and left on the side of the road only to endure and survive all the trauma that comes with poverty, violence, and discrimination.

## Ego Tripping

Let's say you grow up in the Dexter-Linwood neighborhood of Detroit during the late 1980s. Everybody and their uncle has got a job and is making decent money working for Ford or Pontiac or whatever car manufacturer. Then without warning, things change, and a few years later Pops is without work, and your mom left you and your siblings and is nowhere to be seen. Pops doesn't know much about raising children, so he does the best he can in between hanging out with his friends and working odd jobs, but he just ain't around that much to teach you little things like how to make a grilled cheese sandwich. You learn to fend for yourself because you have to help raise your little brother and sister in between visits from your aunties. In high school you learn how to hustle and figure out how to earn money to help pay rent, keep the lights on, and keep your Nikes and hairstyle tight enough to avoid folks from getting into your family's "business."

You've learned how to survive against the odds. A good thing, right? But even though you know how to hustle, you still feel abandoned by your mother. Why did she leave? Even though you know how to "take care of your business," you still feel angry at your father for not being there to show you how to make a grilled cheese sandwich. Now years later, you own a business or direct a large organization, you're successful and powerful, but you still feel abandoned by your parents; you never healed from that shit. So now that you are a leader, you can't let folks know about your abandonment issues, so you hide behind them with a thin veneer of confidence that grows into ego.

We all have versions of that story, when something in our past hurt us and sent us spiraling in some uncharted direction. If we are lucky, we have the opportunity to wrestle with that pain and begin the path of healing. But for most of us, we put that stuff in a brown wooden box, bury it in the basement, and lock the door, trying to forget, just keep it moving. We don't see or recognize the connections between these experiences and how we show up in the world and in our workplaces. But the truth is, it's still there, and because it isn't resolved, it turns into something that's not healthy for ourselves or our work for justice.

Now, I'm not saying that our movements for justice are led by broken people, but rather I'm saying that our leaders haven't always been given the permission to heal. Without healing, ego acts like suspension, saltation, and creep and creates dust storms that cloud decision making. Researchers have studied this process among folks of color, and they call it *racial weathering*. The term refers to the ways that poverty and social, political, and economic exclusion create stress and insecurity, and over time, like paint on a house, they weather away at our health and clarity. Inequality and oppression make some dust storms thicker, longer, and harder to see through than others. In a 2006 study, researchers gauged differences among people in allostatic load, a measure for the wear and tear on the body due to chronic stress. They found a significant difference in allostatic scores between Black and white adults. Blacks in general, and Black women in particular, had the most significant wear and tear on multiple dimensions of their physical and mental health. Researchers concluded that living in a race-conscious society accounted for the undiagnosed stress Blacks and other racial groups experience.[1] Over time, this stress builds up like weather and eventually erodes away at clarity and well-being.

For leaders of color, who day in and day out are forced to weather these dust storms, the only survival tool we may have is our ego. That ego propelled us to get back up again, refusing to surrender no matter how many times we were knocked down. But an ego just isn't a very good tool to use in the middle of a dust storm because it never gets to the root of the problem—it just reacts to it. Clarity comes from both confronting the structural racism that created the conditions for harm and healing the harm itself. Not one or the other, but both. To survive a dust storm, you have to see it first. Ego makes that hard because we can't see beyond ourselves, which makes us oblivious to the real conditions of our lives. Clarity is important for all leaders, but particularly for leaders of color, because without it we cannot see beyond our ego, and therefore we don't even know that a dust storm exists. We cannot work our way to liberation through the obstruction of ego. Mirror work gives us the permission to see the dust storm, prepare for it, and work to get ourselves out of it.

## Lack of Confidence

The second way I've seen leaders lose clarity is by lacking confidence and walking the tightrope of always feeling uncertain. I know, this is almost on the opposite side of the continuum of ego, but it's one important emotional casualty of oppression that I've seen among leaders. From time to time, confidence is something that I've struggled with as well, and it has led to huge clouds of dust particles and lots of blurry, noisy confusion where I could not see.

I suspect that my struggle with confidence came from a phrase my mother would say to me when I would respond to her questions. It's really a story about her confidence, and how her voice was muted and not encouraged to revel in her brilliance. When my mother was in high school in 1959, she was the brightest student in her class. She has shown me her high school report card many times. Yeah, she still keeps her report cards in her bedroom closet, high up on a shelf, in a shoebox stuffed with yellowing prom pictures and postcard-like photos of her and my father in their youth. In one of her favorite classes, she tells me, she had been studying geometry for over a week and, being one of the smartest in the school, was confident about the upcoming test that her teacher, Wilbert Ruffin, was about to give. In preparation for the test, he had asked the class a question, a relatively simple one, and my mother being one of the smartest in the class confidently raised her hand. "Mae, do you have the answer?" Mr. Ruffin said. "Yes sir, I do," my mother replied as she sat up in her seat. What happened next my mother still is recovering from, and to be honest, me too. As she began to explain the answer, with her Southern drawl and small-town Black-girl confidence, Mr. Ruffin abruptly stopped her and said to the class, "It is better to remain silent and be thought a fool than to speak up and remove all doubt." My mother sank deep into her chair with embarrassment as her friends snickered at her. In an instant, the joy and clarity my mother had for learning was taken from her. There goes Mom's confidence and self-assurance, and here comes my battle with self-doubt.

"That stuck with me, Son, I felt humiliated and ashamed of my confidence, like who am I to know the answer. So I started second-guessing everything I said. Instead of speaking up, I just didn't say anything in class anymore. It made me shy, afraid to say what I thought in other parts of my life as well. I just didn't want to feel humiliated like that again."

Growing up, I would be warned of the dangers of "speaking up" and "being thought of as a fool" and the certain humiliation that would come from such an event. So from time to time my mother would repeat this phrase to me, and it has followed me to this very day. At first I didn't really think much about the phrase and the way it impacted my own self-confidence, until I arrived on campus at San Diego State University as an undergraduate student in 1987. My professors in my African American courses cared deeply about cultivating a sense of agency and advocacy within our studies. So they expected us to speak up in class. When I wanted to speak up, however, I could hear a little voice in the back of my mind, "It's better to remain silent than to remove all doubt." So I didn't speak up because I was afraid that I could be wrong and didn't want to be thought of as a fool.

I can see some of these same patterns among leaders of color. I peep it out when leaders are afraid to speak about their bold, courageous vision for their work, or when they don't ask wealthy donors for all the resources they really need. When I've advised amazing leaders of color with fundraising or building relationships with donors, I've heard leaders say to me, "I don't feel comfortable asking for that large an amount of money" or "It's too much to ask someone for." Their comments may come from a sense of modesty or insecurity, but the result is the same, which is a fear-based leadership. Fear-based leadership comes from deep psychic damage to our notions of self-worth, sense of deserving, and perceptions of value. It is rooted in a history of oppression, anchored in structural inequality, and tethered to a legacy of collective harm.

Fear-based leadership basically means that our decisions and actions are created out of fear. This fear has a profound negative impact on us. We ask for less than what we are worth, we second-guess our decisions, and sometimes we just aren't clear when we communicate with others. Fear-based leadership for people of color also comes through the conditioning of oppression that makes us believe that what we have to contribute is not valuable because our movement, style, approach, ideology is counter to or at least different from the institutions we operate within. We shrink to make ourselves and our work less grand because something deep inside of us whispers to us, "Who do you think you are, you can't do that." It's good if we can at least hear that voice, because if we can hear it, we can tell the voice of doubt to shut up and sit down. Unfortunately, most of the time we don't even know that it's there, so we carry on as if it's natural to walk around in the world with doubt, fear, and insecurity and convince ourselves that we are less than who we really are.

Not long ago, a friend who is a recruiter for a large technology company in San Francisco explained to me that when she recruits Black and Latino employees, they almost always accept less salary than white employees. She said her job offers to Black and Latino employees are always 20 to 30 percent less than white candidates with less experience and talent. She explained that when she makes an initial offer to Black and Latino candidates, they almost always accept the first thing she puts on the table, but white candidates feel entitled to ask for much more salary, more stock options, better benefits, and they usually get it!

Research confirms this of course, but don't get it twisted. Wage disparity is not the result of folks of color not feeling confident to ask for more. Wage disparities come from good ole-fashion racism, and there's lots of great research and personal experience to support it. The point is that our confidence is always in question, and that oppression and survival haven't given us the space to stretch out and lean into bold entitlement, which is a feeling of deserved worthiness and the sense that you have the right to ask for what you are worth and need. This sense of entitlement has been one important casualty of oppression. The term *entitlement* usually has been reserved to accurately describe white entitlement, the idea that whiteness and maleness come with unquestioned and unearned special privileges. Like a credit card that grants white folk the benefit of the doubt when they commit crimes or walk into a department store and are welcomed and greeted. White entitlement is an understanding that the world will bend to your own expectation of it simply because you're white. This is invisible to most white folk of course, but most BIPOC folks see it every day.

White entitlement is different than the entitlement that I'm referring to. I'm talking about an "earned" entitlement in a reparations type of way. This just means gaining clarity from the idea that your ancestors have already paid your debt and have picked up the bill. Earned entitlement means gaining a sense of confidence and clarity from a deep understanding of what it cost your ancestors to bring you to this point. Reminding yourself of the forced removal of Native nations, and how land was stolen from the Seminole and Cherokee, can provide Native and Indigenous leaders with earned entitlement through an understanding that they deserve higher pay, better benefits, and more stock options not only because they have value but also because of the back pay owed to their ancestors. Research has estimated that nearly one million Black families have lost over 12 million acres of land from sanctioned federal and corporate land schemes. Earned entitlement comes with a reminder that you have a right to ask for what you're worth. There is a phrase in Maya Angelou's poem "Still I Rise" that says, "Bringing the gifts that my ancestors gave, I am the dream and the hope of the slave."

Sometimes, when I'm feeling insecure, uncertain, and unclear, I remind myself that "I am the hope and the dream of the slave," and I ask myself, "What would make me worthy of my ancestor's dream in this situation?" I imagine my grandfather William Ginwright and his father, Homus Ginwright, sitting together on a porch in their overalls, overlooking the expansive land they owned in North Carolina. They are proud of what they have worked for, and their hands like my father's hands are worn and leathery from working the soil. I imagine them saying to me in a gentle and humble way, "You got this, and you can't fail cuz we done already paved the way for you, Son, all you gotta do is walk." Then, when I play that scene over in my head, I feel the power of their wisdom and courage of their journey to move with earned entitlement and clarity.

## A Challenge with Resistance

The third way that leaders of color lose clarity is by seeing themselves and their work only through the lens of opposition and resistance. Sometimes leaders get stuck into a way of only seeing the world through the lens of "anti" and therefore limit their work's full potential. From time to time, my students at San Francisco State University, arguably one of the most liberal places in the world, proclaim during class that they are "anti . . ." fill in the blank (racist, sexist, homophobic, colonial, and so on). While it's important to take a stance against systems that reinforce subjugation, it's simply not enough to define our work by what it is in opposition to. Usually, I explain to my students that an ocean is not anti-land, nor is water anti-air. Love is not anti-hate, nor is courage anti-fear. A chair is not an anti-table, because these are objects with meaning, definition, function, and purpose in themselves. They don't need to be defined in relationship to something else. When we name something as simply the opposition of what it is not, that does little to affirm our full humanity and create the world we seek as leaders. It means that our work is inextricably defined, and therefore limited, by the very thing we wish to transform. When we define ourselves and our work in this way, we limit ourselves because we are so much more than the opposite of what we seek to eliminate.

It's not enough to engage in transformative, healing-centered change and believe that it can occur by referring to our work as "opposition" to oppression. Leaders need to go a few steps beyond and name what we wish to see rather than what we need to resist. This is not a simple play with words but rather a way that leaders of color sometimes become blinded and simply cannot fully see the world they want to create. Take for instance the term *anti-racist*. While an anti-racist stance and view of the world are important for rejecting racism, the term fails to claim and affirm what we truly want: belonging. Do we want to live in an anti-racist society or a society based in belonging? I'm not splitting hairs here, because the terms we use to describe our work matter in how we do it and how we show up. My goal for all my students is to get to a place where they define themselves and their work from a place of both affirmation and necessary resistance. While this mindset shift is important, the harder work that leaders need to embrace is cultivating the vision to see the end result and naming it even when it seems impossible. It's not easy to see a society based in belonging when all of our institutions close ranks, cater to the privileged, and reject the poor. Our job as leaders, however, is to seek clarity even in the midst of a dust storm.

Clarity allows leaders to confidently answer the question, What are you creating? We know what you resist, but what are you building? These questions get at the heart of clarity because in the fight for justice we often become so absorbed in resisting oppression and confronting injustice that we lose sight of the beloved community we really wish to create. For those of us who have been involved in social justice work for most of our lives, we know the bewildered feeling that comes with a campaign victory. We've worked so long to end youth prisons, and then suddenly, the state or city decides to end funding for youth prisons and support alternatives to youth incarceration. Turns out that in some cases, organizing groups haven't focused enough on what system could be created in its place.

There is a verse in the Bible that says something like faith is the substance of things hoped for, the evidence of things not seen. This gets at the heart of what clarity is, and why it's important for leaders to engage in the relentless practice of creating clarity for ourselves and for our movements. Our movements need to move people to another way of seeing in the world and cultivate a culture of possibility. Clarity helps us see the dust storm ahead of us, and reminds us to slow down, stay calm when we are in it, and keep our vision on our destination. It's not easy to stay calm in a dust storm or slow down when we are in the swirling, twirling clouds of confusion and uncertainty. This is why clarity is an ongoing practice, not an ultimate destination. From time to time, we'll get confused, wander from the path we began, and fall into the frenzy of confusion. When that happens, you don't need to beat yourself up—just recognize what's happening, brush off the dust, remember where you want to go, and get back on the road.

## CLEAR AS A BELL

Suspension, saltation, and creep are always present to some degree in our lives and in our work. These dust storms come disguised as internal conflicts in our organizations, structural racism in our cities, and divisiveness in our nation. But it's hard to fight with dust in your eyes, and it's even harder to know where to go when you can't see. So how do we gain clarity when most of the time we work and live in some degree of a dust storm? My own research and experience says that clarity is a journey more than a destination, and with a few simple practices we can cultivate the skills that can help with our own clarity and can contribute to the clarity of our movements for justice. Both are inextricably connected and bound by each other.

To get clear, sometimes I review some of my favorite authors, who, when I flip through the pages of books I have read, offer insight and direction on important questions about life, justice, and movement building. I have a tendency to review notes I've taken and highlighted in books written by Howard Thurman, James Baldwin, and Grace Lee Boggs. They all have a profound way to describe the relationship between individual and society, personal and political, healing and movements. I think one lesson that I can take from my refuge into their writings is that there is a relationship between our inner work and our social and political work. Transforming our communities and building a more just society require that we all recognize the ways that oppression has made it difficult to take seriously the inner work required for social change.

Here are a few ways that we can develop the practice of clarity in our lives and in our work. These are not meant to be a step-by-step recipe to obtain clarity, but rather a guide that can help us recognize the dust storm and lead us through it. Remember that this is a practice, which means sometimes you'll do well and other times you won't. The most important thing is that we engage and remain consistent. Over time, with practice, these habits can help us all see more clearly when things get out of control and confusing.

## Slow Down and Let the Dust Settle

Most of the time, when we are working on some project or trying to achieve a particular goal, we run into patches of confusion and uncertainty. When that happens, we have the tendency to make decisions and move forward because of our timeline and an urgency to plow through. During times of uncertainty, it is important to regain clarity by first slowing down and letting go of the pressure to "get it right." When we do that, we let the dust settle, which gives us the time to regain focus and determine what's most important. Slowing down, of course, isn't something that we embrace in our society because our values have been shaped by capitalist culture, which emphasizes efficiency and expedience. Slowing down means that we give ourselves and our work permission to take more time to reflect, think, ponder, and imagine.

In some of my work leading groups through racial equity training, one of the first activities requires that each person share their personal history and story with the entire group. Depending on the size of the group, this can take up a good chunk of time. After we do this, however, the entire group has so much clarity about who is in the room and where the group is heading. Slowing down also means simply recognizing when you don't know what to do. When that happens, I take a walk and try to sort things out or take a pause in my work to regain focus.

Sometimes I ask these questions:

► What is unclear, and what am I not seeing?

► What is most important right now in this moment?

► Is my ego making this unclear?

► What do I most fear in this situation, and why?

► What would my mentor do in this situation?

Asking ourselves and the groups we lead questions like these can help us slow down just enough to let the dust settle and regain or create our clarity.

## Create a Purpose-Driven Outcome

I'm always amazed how difficult it is for people to clearly talk about their goals or desired outcomes when it comes to their personal life and their work. I suspect that most of us don't really spend much time thinking about our personal or professional goals because survival has become the default. Perhaps one of the most important practices we can use in gaining clarity is determining what our goal and desired outcome should be. Most of my students, when I have them describe a desired outcome, usually reply, "We want justice / better schools / police accountability." But when I ask them to identify its specific characteristics, things get blurry. In order to cultivate clarity, we have to get unambiguous about the goals and explicit about the outcomes we want to achieve. When we get specific about the outcomes of our work for social and racial justice, for example, we may determine the goal is to make ethnic studies a required subject in high school in your state.

More important is taking the time to see the big picture and final destination and not getting lost in the journey. This could be hard because things are always changing, and there are new issues that need to be addressed every day. But when we dig deep and clear away all the debris that makes it hard to connect with the deeper purpose of our work, we gain a spiritual drive to walk every day in our path toward that goal. Write down what your purpose is, note the concrete steps you can take to support it, and remind yourself of what you have been called to do in our collective work toward a better society.

## Practice Consistently and Faithfully

More than anything else, it is important to create a consistent and faithful practice of reminding ourselves who we are, what our purpose is, and where we want to go. This doesn't mean that we all need to enroll in a theology class or visit a monastery (though these experiences would definitely help build clarity with consistent practice), but all it requires is for us to regularly wrestle with the questions that help with our clarity. A friend of mine commented not long ago, "The only way out is in," and when he said this it surprised me because he's not the type that believes in the importance of the inner journey to justice. He doesn't really see the nexus between personal transformation and social change, self-reflection and public action. But in his own way, he actually does recognize the limits of transactional ways of changing our society. His comment pointed to an important truth in our quest for a more just society, which is that our self-reflection and mirror work allow us to cultivate the clarity we need to heal ourselves, and to have faith that our actions, no matter how big or small, will create the society we want.

# Pivot 2

## From Transactional to Transformative

# 4

# *Belonging*

*The wrong first question is, What do we need to do?*
*The right first question is, Who do we need to become?*

BENJAMIN MCBRIDE

The Little Pee Dee River in North Carolina is full of mosquitos in the summer, and in August the air is thick, hot, and steamy. The river meanders 116 miles through the South Carolina woods and is a tributary to its larger cousin, the Big Pee Dee River. At dusk, when the sun hangs low and orange in the sky, right before the orchestra of crickets, beetles, and frogs begin their cacophonous performance, you can see fireflies near the edge of the water, skirting, bouncing, and hovering in clusters of glowing wonder. The river is mostly blackwater, dark and shallow, sometimes flowing slowly into swampland. The river is named from the Pee Dee American Indians, who have occupied this land for thousands of years. If you listen, sometimes you can hear the river flowing, but most of the time it's a quiet and sleepy river that takes long naps in the cool shade underneath the canopy of trees above.

The first time I heard of the Pee Dee River was in the summer of 1979. I was lying on the floor of my aunt's house, playing with the fan, trying to stay cool. My father, William Jr., and his sister Sylvia had conspired to bring their father and his brother to Riverside, California, for a few weeks to spend time with the family. William Sr., my grandfather, and his brother lived in Jacksonville, Florida, for most of their lives and had raised seven children. My grandfather was soft spoken, gentle, and didn't talk much. He always wore a clean white-collared cotton shirt, neatly ironed dress slacks, and a brown belt. When it was hot, rather than putting on a T-shirt or a tank top, he would just roll up his sleeves and pull the handkerchief from his pocket to dab the beads of sweat that gathered on his brow. He was church-going, proud, and humble. He worked with his hands his entire life and had taught my father how to fix, repair, and build just about anything. His brother, on the other hand, was quite the opposite. Uncle "Buck," my grandfather's brother, loved to tell stories and took every opportunity to say exactly what was on his mind. They were close, inseparable, and best of friends.

I don't know exactly why my father decided to grab his old tape recorder that afternoon to record his father and uncle recount the Ginwright family history, but I'm glad he did. For three hours, my brothers and I sat on the floor and listened to my grandfather and his brother share amazing stories about their childhood. They recounted tales, argued about irrelevant facts, and most importantly explained to us how our family had owned over 1,500 acres of land between the Big Pee Dee and Little Pee Dee Rivers in Marion County, South Carolina. They belonged to the land, and all their fond memories of growing up and learning to farm, hunt, and fish were nurtured on that land. They laughed and rejoiced sharing stories about their own grandfather, Homus Ginwright, who taught them to hunt, fish, and tend to the sheep that grazed their land. At one time, the Ginwrights had a community school, a store, and land in a vibrant community. We aren't exactly sure what happened to all that land; as Uncle Buck recalled, "We were run off our land by white folks." He shared a story about how whites from the nearby town had over the years used violence and illegal property schemes to take control of the family's land. Hearing the account by my grandfather and Uncle Buck wasn't just new to me, it was also the first time my father had ever heard of Homus Ginwright, the land our family had owned, and how we lost it. It was in that moment that I felt a sense of deep belonging to a kinship longer and stronger than I could have ever imagined.

This may have been a new feeling for me, but kinship has always been important to my mother. From time to time when I talk to my mother, she will give me the latest news about her side of the family. When someone gets married, passes away, graduates from college, or relocates, she'll begin the conversation with an elaborate genealogical mapping of precisely who the story is about. She'll say, "You know your cousin Hank on my momma's side of the family? The one who was the first in our family to go off to college and he married that sweet girl from Chicago?" I'll reply, "I don't think I know him, Momma," at which time she'll say, "Oh yes you do, he is my uncle's first son on my momma's side of the family." For my mother, it's important to know where you came from and where you belong. You gotta know your kinfolk, my mother always reminded me. Sometimes I have to admit that I get a little irritated when she introduces me to a distant cousin (grandfather's brother's auntie's son on her father's side) whom I have never met. When she introduces me, it's awkward because she expects that our kinfolk connection should invoke an immediate bonding experience. I feel guilty when that happens because I don't feel that type of immediate kinship connection that my mother has with her cousins. But I've come to appreciate her efforts to keep me and my brothers connected to our kinfolk because even if we don't have an initial spark, I recognize the importance of the unspoken bond that we share, and how those bonds help shape who we are.

## BELONGING AS HUMAN KINSHIP

*Kinship* is the deep sense of feeling connected to a history, people, and place to which you belong. It is a sacred bond that anchors relationships among people. Kin, kinship, kinfolk, next of kin, kindred are all forms of belonging to a people, place, and history that give meaning to our lives. Kinship is a bond and binding relationship that occurs without consent. I had no choice or decision about who my brothers would be, yet we are still kin. I didn't consent to or select my parents or grandparents, yet I'm bound to a patrilineal and matrilineal relationship to them. Belonging is different because it requires mutual consent to matter to one another. *Belonging* is a mutual exchange of care, compassion, and courage that binds people together in a way that says you matter. It means that because you are a human being, you have the ordained right to be a member of this group.

Belonging, unlike kinship, requires agreement among groups to form meaningful connection and purposeful membership. Belonging provides us with an identity, a sense of meaning, connection, and purpose. It happens when we join clubs in college, civic groups to solve tough problems in our cities, and movements that improve the conditions of our society. Most of us have experienced a sense of deep connectedness with others in our faith communities or in support groups. These types of spaces provide a container for sharing, vulnerability, and listening, which are all important ingredients for belonging.

African Americans have had deep and rich forms of kinship, but an odd and distant relationship to belonging in America. The traumatic history of the Atlantic slave trade, the advent of chattel slavery, the structure of white supremacy and racial inequality, and persistent state-sanctioned racial violence on Black communities all have served as a clear declaration that Black folk don't belong in America. Even my own family's land, the place where my grandfather was raised and belonged in the Brittons Neck area of Marion County, South Carolina, was stolen over the years. A white family had killed and run off many of the Ginwrights. This is just one small and tragic story in a history of not belonging.

The history of not belonging is enshrined in America's DNA. Just read Ta-Nehisi Coates's *A Case for Reparations* or Ibram X. Kendi's work about the history of racist ideas in America. Together both Coates and Kendi weave together the brutal and honest truth about racism and not belonging in the same way James Baldwin taught us forty years ago. Not belonging is a particularly important reality for leaders of color, and we haven't given ourselves permission to heal from the wounds that come with not belonging. When we are wounded from not belonging, our sacred connections are severed, and we are cut off from the power of human connection. In order for leaders to form durable transformative relationships, healing from not belonging is one of the most important first steps.

## BECOMING, BELONGING, AND JUSTICE

Ben McBride grew up in a yellow house on a steep hill in the Hunters Point district of San Francisco. His parents were solid middle-class and worked hard to make sure their six children had everything they needed to succeed. His house smelled and felt like church. Downstairs, on the wall next to the kitchen, there were pictures of Jesus on the cross, a child decked in a white robe being baptized in a small pond, two children praying together with their hands clasped tightly. Above the fireplace mantel, there were two large praying hands, complemented by a large red and black Bible on the coffee table. His father was a deacon in the church in their neighborhood.

In the 1980s Hunters Point was full of youthful joy. Kids running in and out of each other's homes, playing double Dutch outside until the streetlights came on. Ben and his friends would ride their bikes to the corner store to buy a Snickers candy bar and rush home to watch someone's pirated videotape of an HBO movie. There was a communal sense of joy and a deep sense of belonging in all of that.

As his neighborhood changed, so did Ben, but his sense of community and belonging remained intact. He attended his best friend's funeral when he was just sixteen. At St. John Missionary Baptist Church on Third Street, there were hundreds of teenage Black kids crying at the funeral; they couldn't believe that they had lost Antwan. He commented, "I remember the confusion of that day and trying to make sense of it all. I just remember that sense of community. We didn't have a lot of answers, but we had each other."

Ben believes deep down in his bones that healing how we belong is the only way to transform our society. He says that the harm that comes from not belonging has inflicted a deep wound that we cannot even see. We have all experienced times of not belonging. For many of us, that may have been a substantial portion of our middle or high school experience as we grew to find ourselves and our voice. Think back to your freshman year of high school or even college. Did you experience some weeks of eating alone before you met that special friend? How did it feel to sit alone? It's really hard to feel like you just don't belong to anyone or any group. Maybe if you did fit in right away, it was because you went to school with friends you had known for some time—how did it feel to have their support that first week of school? To know that you never had to walk the hallways alone and had other people who shared your common goals and interests is what it means to belong. Yet this wound of not belonging influences everything we do and how we see the world. Our goal is to heal these wounds in order to transform and evolve and become a better version of ourselves. Ben's ideas about belonging were formed in the crucible of being raised in the church and from being in close proximity to what was happening in the hood.

As an adult, Ben's ideas about belonging grew as he began to lead campaigns to address police violence in Black communities. His insight came from a deep frustration and fatigue of trying to "beat evil with evil or trying to defeat hate with hate." Protest after protest and demonstration after demonstration and ongoing political battles started to change him into someone he no longer recognized. He realized that he was becoming the very thing he detested.

Ben commented when I interviewed him,

*I've been finding that organizers are starting to come to the end of their journey around what their work is all supposed to be adding up to. People are burning out because the way that we're trying to go about engaging with the world is eating away at our soul and is eating away at our consciousness. Our work doesn't refill us, it exploits, it extracts, it does not fuel us. I realized that I was becoming the very thing that I abhorred. You know, in order to stop police from dehumanizing Black people, I started dehumanizing police. This way of thinking was wearing me down. I realized that I had to become something different in order to live into the value that I felt of wanting to be connected in a different way.*

Belonging for Ben was a deeply self-reflective process that took lots of practice of trial and error. He realized that belonging required deep change and transformation of his assumptions and how he showed up for others. It was easy to practice belonging with the young Black men he was organizing, but how to practice belonging with police who openly disdain young Black men seemed impossible but necessary. Being a novice means that you become humble and curious about what you don't know. It means discovering aspects of yourself that you didn't realize existed. For Ben, it meant trying to connect to young Black men by talking about Jesus and realizing that his approach didn't resonate with them. Next he tried to be a father figure and realized that wasn't creating a connection either. But the lesson was in the journey. He realized that belonging was a practice that required relentless self-examination, constant questioning, and persistent learning to transform himself into someone that could expand his notions of belonging.

His most significant pivot to belonging came when he went to Ferguson, Missouri, to join the protest and organizing for Black lives. He commented,

*Ferguson was another one of those big shifts where I had to become somebody different. You know, up until that point, I had never protested a day in my life. I remember when the young brothers told me in Ferguson, "Come on, big bruh, come get in the street with us." I immediately was like, "I'm not getting in the street!" I heard my dad's voice in the back of my head saying, "We don't get in the streets, we do incremental change. This is not what we do." I'm looking at these young brothas and they*

*got tattoos on their face and got no shirts on! So all of my biases*
*that I didn't even know I had, kicked in. I said to myself, "I'm not*
*about to get in the street with you. My wife is gonna kill me, I got*
*three girls at home!" All my bourgeois negro sensibilities were*
*kicking in. But I realized in that moment, that if I want to con-*
*nect with y'all, I need to be here with y'all. I have to follow your*
*invitation; I have to trust. If we really want to find a different*
*outcome, we're gonna have to be willing to really give ourselves*
*to a different process.*

His lesson wasn't an intellectual exercise but a deeply heartfelt
awakening. He realized that if he wanted to cultivate belonging, he
also would have to become a better version of himself.

## WHO SHOULD WE BECOME?

McBride's lesson for those of us who have dedicated our lives to social
change is that we have to transform ourselves before we can create the
world we imagine. There are two views of transformative change: the
old-world view and the new-world view. The old-world view of social
change focuses entirely on building the power that's necessary to exert
influence over people, processes, and events. Building power is the cornerstone of organizing because it is based in fostering relationships,
cultivating trust, creating collective awareness needed to vote, march,
voice an opinion on any given topic. Power building is important, and
no movements for justice would have been possible without the power
that has come for mobilizing people to act. But the old-world view of
change also has its limits and comes with a social emotional cost to our
ability to cultivate belonging. As a result of our unhealed pain, we close
ranks and build solidarity with like-minded people. This is important
for our collective healing, but in the process we begin to "other" those
outside of our groups. *Othering* is the tendency to assign negative attributes to groups of people other than your own.

Othering is rooted in the inclination of humans to live and organize themselves in social groups. We do this by forming meaningful connections with others based on family, religion, race, gender,

language, and nationality, for example. When this happens, we form positive attributes for members of our "tribe" (us); for those who are not in our social group (them), we identify as "not belonging" and assign negative attributes to that group. Over time, we begin to perceive differences between in-group "us" and out-group "them," which results in polarization, the relative strength of our perceived differences. This happens with race, class, gender, gender identity, sexuality, nationality, and just about any difference you can think about. Researchers suggest that the process of forming tribes is a function of evolution.[1] When small groups of people were forced to survive and compete over scarce resources, tribalism was beneficial—banding together was advantageous for survival. Banding together also came with a sense of safety, rules, and norms that over time functioned as a collective identity. Some researchers argue that the tendency to identify with a group is enshrined in our DNA.[2] Others claim that this collective identity, or tribal identity, determined who was good and who was bad, who to share with and who not to share with. These decisions were a means of survival.

In a recent study, researchers wanted to test how our tendency to form tribes influenced perceptions of in-group (us) and out-group (them) members.[3] They randomly selected 100 people and asked them to indicate group categories such as country of citizenship and sports team. They entered the participants in a simulated game and asked them to determine how much they think another person should be punished for breaking the rules of the game. They found that people generally punished out-group categories more harshly than their own in-group. Similar findings have been noted with children as young as age six. Researchers published in the journal of the US National Academy of Sciences found that children tend to punish out-group more than in-group members for the same mistake. They assigned children ages six to eight to a blue team or yellow team. Through simulated play, the researchers asked the children to either share their candy or remove candy from the other children. They found that the children were more likely to share candy with their in-group and remove candy from out-group members.[4]

This process is precisely what happened to Ben as he organized for police reform. His own brother, Pastor Michael McBride, had been violently beaten by the police while attending theological seminary. Ben had developed a strong in-group identity and had bred a strong animosity and disdain for police officers, the out-group. His feelings toward the police were of course justified as he had witnessed firsthand the violence police officers had unleashed in Black communities, as well as the corruption, cover-ups, and the gross protection law enforcement enjoyed.

Ben had become so consumed in his hatred of police that one day he realized that his disdain, disgust, and animosity had made him sick. He had become physically, mentally, and spiritually ill and exhausted. He began to question not so much what he was advocating for (police accountability, demilitarization of law enforcement, community-driven solutions to community safety) but how he was going about these goals. He began to question what his real goal was in organizing and what it really meant to "win" a campaign. Was it to gain power over those institutions that cause harm, or was it to sit on the new throne of power to punish those that had harmed our communities?

His questions forced him to rethink his approach to justice, because he was tired of being sick and tired. He realized that the very sickness that sustained white supremacy in law enforcement was the same sickness that had bred his disdain for law enforcement, which was precisely the inability for him or them to see each other as human. McBride commented,

> *We are trying to go about creating change that is transactional instead of transformative. This type of thinking assumes that, somehow, the current version of ourselves can actually give birth to something different in our society. Sometimes leaders don't really understand what the real "win" would mean. We need to redefine what it means to win, and the present version of ourselves we just cannot see. But a deeper, more enlightened version of ourselves that we can begin to envision.*

But what does it mean to reimagine the meaning of winning? What does it mean to become a more enlightened version of our-selves? These questions get to the heart of the new-world view of transformative change. The new-world view of change is not simply about winning but more importantly involves focusing on how we make change and who we become in the process. In our journey for justice, how we get there is just as important as the destination; the two cannot be separated.

There is an ongoing debate among social justice leaders about old-world vs. new-world social change. For old-world leaders and orga-nizers, voting, mobilizing the base, and movement building are the only real levers of power. Power in the old-world view is considered a form of capital that can be deployed in order to exert influence on people, events, and institutions. Researchers of social movements, for example, have called this form of power *resource mobilization* to indicate how social change occurs. Sociologists argue that social movements are largely a function of mobilizing resources like people, money, and ideas to shape distribution of power, a classic old-world view of social change.[5]

Other social justice leaders view change from the new-world perspective, which focuses on the quality of our vision, the depth of our relationships, and our ability to cultivate belonging. This is not to say that old-world views of change are irrelevant—quite the contrary. New-world leaders understand the significance of tacti-cal power but also recognize its limits. New-world power is based in the capacity to foster and sustain a beloved community, a sense of belonging, and human connection even with those who are in your out-group (them). These ideas about social change are actually not really "new." In fact, Howard Thurman wrote over fifty years ago about the power of belonging in our quest for justice and social change. He wrote in an essay titled "Luminous Darkness,"

> *Laws are limited in that they can only establish the climate*
> *(rules) for fellowship (civil society), but they are limited in that*
> *they cannot guarantee the spiritual and moral requisites of a*

*(beloved) community. This work must happen over time with a process of moral practices that cultivate a climate of grace and compassion. Without this, we are only building the symbols of a great society.[6]*

As we see in Thurman's work, and through other scholars as well, the term *new world* might not be entirely accurate, but I think you get the point. Which is exactly what McBride realized when he decided to pivot to another way to seek social change. In responding to old-world views of power and social change, McBride explained,

*Yes, we need the power! Yes, we need to be able to hold people accountable. But how we go about getting to accountability, how we go about getting that power is as important as the actual power itself and specific results that we get. If we go to get those things, by becoming them, we will replace them. What's the point of going to the promised land if you become Pharaoh on your sojourn? You will have changed everything and changed absolutely nothing. The real point is not just about getting to the promised land, the point is about arriving to the promised land as the beautiful people that we are coming out of oppression. So how we get there and where we ultimately get to cannot be disconnected.*

Let the church say . . . Amen! Ben's concern is that social justice leaders become so consumed by the pursuit of winning that they simply replace the oppressor, leaving the existing deeper values in place (us versus them). Another element that Ben uplifts is the emotional toll that the journey and fight take on us. When combined with the existing trauma caused by oppression we deal with, this process can only create a leader who replaces an oppressor's trauma with their own. In order to truly transform our society and create a new way, we have to become a better version of ourselves. Only when we pursue this path, and trust and believe that there is another way, can we create something more beautiful and different. Ben has coined a phrase to capture the essence of becoming and belonging:

*The wrong first question is, What do we need to do? The right first question is, Who do we need to become?*

McBride admits that he is still becoming and that he is still learning and growing into the person he wants to be.

*I'm someone who lives in the liminal space of not being where I was and not quite being where I want to be. I think I'm becoming more open, less angry, and more loving. I'm still working on getting my intellectual chops to actually figure out how to chart a pathway there. But my capacity to imagine a different society has grown. My capacity to believe that people who are on the wrong side of history can get on the right side of history has grown.*

So, what has Ben's journey looked like as he's worked to become the person he wants to be? McBride's own awareness of becoming began when he was trying to figure out how to support young brothas who were involved in gun violence. He realized that people can do things that are so against who they are at the core because of their fears, anxiety, and trauma. The young Black men involved with gun violence all had deep traumatic experiences that shaped their decisions on the surface, but who they were at the core remained unscathed. If someone is willing to see these young men as human, even when they show up with inhumane behavior, it affords these young men the ability to act from their core rather than as the person that society has conditioned them to be. He has experienced this transformation so many times with young Black men that he came to realize that the same must be possible for those groups of people he had come to disdain and reject. He realized that if it's possible for these young Black men who use guns to solve their problems to transform, it must also be possible for someone who works in the police department to change as well. McBride agrees that the system of policing is a racist system, but the human beings in that system are not the system itself. Just like the human beings involved in gun violence, who are victims of the system, are not the system itself.

They are people who find themselves in dehumanizing situations. In order to transform the system, the people in those systems have to transform.

McBride began to use this way of thinking in all his work after a training with the Santa Monica Police Department. He had spent a day training police officers about implicit bias, structural racism, and racial equity. After his training, one of the officers pulled him to the side and wanted to talk with him privately. The officer was white, in her midthirties, and when she spoke to him, she was stern, clear, and precise. Her hair was pulled back, neatly gathered in a bun, and her blue-rimmed eyeglasses made her look a bit like a college professor. The officer confided in McBride and passionately shared with him. "I was falsely accused of doing something improper, and there are so many unjust things happening in our department," she explained to him. "I internalized that, you know, and I felt really bad and unfairly treated when that happened. So after that, I just said fuck it, you know, I'm gonna let things happen. If people are doing something wrong, I'm not gonna say anything because I was falsely accused, and it hurt me deep." During the training, McBride had led the officers through a series of activities, sharing opportunities, and key lessons about belonging. He shared with the officers that "we have to become better versions of ourselves in order to transform the system." She explained to McBride that when she heard him say that, "I felt something that I was holding on to break off inside of me, as I thought about what could be." As she was speaking to Ben, she paused, her voice softened, and she began to cry.

It was a moment of vulnerability where for an instant the officer's humanity spilled out. Ben placed his arm around the officer to offer comfort and to let her know that it was OK in that moment for her to be human. She continued explaining to Ben, "I don't want to be the cop that I've been and that they've trained me to be, I want to be somebody different." It was as if she had discovered something in her that she had forgotten. McBride realized that with the right kind of cultivation and investment of time, people can grow into the kinds of leaders we need that can ultimately transform policing. Over and over, his experience with white evangelicals, police, or shooters has shown him that people on the wrong side of history can change and that these people are needed for the systemic structural change we ultimately need.

## PEOPLE NEED TO BE SEEN

Have you ever noticed what happens when two Black people first see each other or walk by each other, even if they are complete strangers? They softly glance at each other and slightly nod their heads as a sign of acknowledgment to say "I see you." This gesture comes from the Zulu greeting *sawubona*, which means "I see you," and in response *yebo, sawubona*, which means "we see you." This is a sacred greeting that acknowledges the ancestral meaning of what it means to be seen and to belong. The greeting is a sort of dialogue between people that establishes that one is a witness to someone else's presence. It is a gesture that we see each other and affirms the reality that we are connected and offers an invitation to participate in a mutual existence. Orland Bishop, spiritual leader and director of the ShadeTree Multicultural Foundation in Los Angeles, uses the concept of *sawubona* to help us all answer perhaps the most important question we need to ask ourselves, "How do I have to be as a human being for someone else to be free?"

This question gets at the heart of McBride's statement, "The wrong first question is, What do we need to do? The right first question is, *Who do we need to become?*" Fundamental shifts in our society require that we all wrestle with these questions and struggle to find the answers. It's not so much coming up with the perfect, concise, neatly wrapped response as much as jumping into the conflicting, messy, confusing, and worthy pursuit of answering these questions. McBride shared his own messy journey into becoming.

*You know, I've trained hundreds of police officers around the country in New York, in DC and California, in Oregon and Washington, and I've seen the same thing happen. I've worked*

*with young brothers all across the country and I've seen the*
*same thing happen. This just suggests to me that another world*
*is possible.*

It may have not been so much an epiphany as it was yet another
data point. His experiences with shooters and the police were the
same. Given the right conditions, people can change. But this is a
hard sell to social change advocates who see change only through the
lens of old-world strategies, which view change through the lens of
power and resource mobilization. The problem is that this old-world
view is based in scarcity and fear, and therefore we commodify everything ranging from people to time. We tell ourselves that there is not
enough time to treat human beings like human beings because we're
experiencing pain. We convince ourselves that there are not enough
resources to do it because of scarcity, so all we can do is what we
have always done, dehumanize others so we can get relief. But that
is how the system actually perpetuates itself. As McBride explains,
"We're trying to beat their dehumanization of us with dehumanizing
them. This just creates a cycle of more dehumanization."

The systems that we have created are destroying our capacity
to live in our full humanity. Not only for students and teachers in
schools, but also child welfare, social work, medical professionals,
and law enforcement. But any system that fails to center the humanity of people will ultimately erode our capacity to belong. McBride
recalls training with the Oakland Police Department, and an officer
shared with him that he had recently walked into a murder scene
with eight dead bodies and blood and guts dripping from the wall.
The officer described a graphic scene and the emotional toll it took
on him. When the officer walked into the police department, he faced
a culture where if you need mental health support, you are laughed
at and ridiculed. The officer said, "So we just go home every day
without processing all the shit we see every day. I drove home that
day in silence. When I got home, I sat down, and my girlfriend said,
'How was work?' And all I said to her was 'fine.'"

The system is destroying him mentally, emotionally, and spiritually. Yet we are asking him to show up in our community in a

way that he is not able to because the system is not showing up for him. The same can be said when we are asking Black young people to show up to school in a way that they sometimes are not able to because the school isn't showing up for them. Yet we demonize these same people because we feel like we don't have enough time to support their full humanity. If we stop or at least slow down, we can see that there is something deeper that needs to shift. It's like we are constantly patching these systems with tape and hoping that they can actually support full human belonging. There is this false idea that we can transform our systems without transforming the people who are in them. We spend so much time and resources on all of the externalities of these systems, like the policies, rules, procedures, but the people in those systems haven't fundamentally changed, yet we expect better outcomes. We all need to pivot to deeper, more transformative ways to connect and belong.

## DON'T BE IN LOVE WITH A BEAUTIFUL LIE

This is the time for us all to realize that there is another way. The systems and structures of our society were created out of individualism, fear, and scarcity, and they can be refashioned based in collectivity, love, and abundance. But it takes our collective imagination and capacity to cultivate belonging with both our in-groups and out-groups. This is tough work because it requires that we first do some deep soul searching within ourselves. Before we can hold others accountable, we have to hold ourselves accountable and work on areas of our lives where we need to do better. A pivot to transformative relationships begins with restoring the relationship with ourselves. This means that we have to sit with the question, Who have I been, and what has it cost me or my relationships with others? When we sit with questions like this, it forces us to lean into the messiness of life and uncover the ways that we lie to ourselves and believe that our growth is fixed and our healing is limited. We will also need to sit in community and cultivate the courage to extend our circle of belonging. Extending our circle of belonging won't be easy because it will go against everything we believe about how change happens. Extending our circle of belonging will also raise some important questions for our work. Why do we have to hold the work of belonging? How does belonging hold others accountable? How does belonging change the fundamental systems that harm us?

McBride reminds us that while these questions are important, they lull us into falling in love with a beautiful lie. The beautiful lie is that there is only one way to achieve our dream of justice, and that we will "win" if we fight the enemy harder, resist oppression with more vigor, confront injustice with more strength. While these actions are important, we also have to attend to a way of being that can shift the deeper values upon which our society is built. Practicing belonging is perhaps one of the most radical acts of justice simply because it pulls the blanket off and reveals the hidden ways that capitalist culture, white supremacy, and individualism govern the very logic of how we imagine and think about social change. We've been conditioned and socialized in ways to overvalue our own experience and discount or undervalue the experience of others. We believe that how we see the world is how the world is seen. When we act, think, and engage only from our own perspective, it becomes nearly impossible to create belonging across difference. Our experiences are sacred, and we should celebrate that, but when we want to create belonging, as McBride says, "We have to be willing to start a new journey with other people, and engage in different conversations with deep listening and not assume that we know the answers, 'I know what should be done based upon the experience that I've had.'" He encourages us to embrace the courage to learn and listen not for agreement but from a place of humble curiosity and the possibility of belonging.

But how do we cultivate belonging among those responsible for George Floyd's death? As a Black man, how do I create space to be curious about white supremacy? What value is there in expanding a sense of belonging when so many Black people are hurting and locked out of America's promise? There is deep spiritual work we all need to do to build our capacity to create belonging even in the midst of so much unjust suffering. McBride shared a story about an incident during a meeting when he came face to face with a police officer who had been acquitted for shooting a Black young man. When I asked McBride how he could meet with a police officer that had killed a Black man and gotten away with it, he replied:

*What enabled me to do that was that I had to practice how I would speak to myself. I did a lot of self-reflection that enabled me to enter that conversation with a lower stress. I would try to imagine the nine- or ten-year-old boy inside those white officers in front of me. I would think how much they must have lost with their own humanity, and then became sick and violent and angry and racist. I would say to myself this is what is expressing itself when they show up in our neighborhoods. It's not so much how you prepare yourself just to show up in those kinds of conversations but more about how to be in the world.*

We all have the capacity for belonging with people who have done terrible things. It's our proximity to them that determines our ability to see their humanity or not. Our proximity and capacity to get close to others give us the handles to work on our ability to create belonging across difference. It's not easy but may be the only way to pivot to transformative values in our society. We may have not realized the full potential of what it means to be a human being and live in community with one another. We are still desperately trying to figure this out, but for the most part this journey has been shaped by violence and power. Perhaps we need to take a longer view of belonging that shifts our collective gaze into a possible future. Maybe belonging isn't something that we do as a quick-fix strategy to gain racial equity or redress racial oppression. Rather, it requires that we take a longer view of how to achieve transformative change. As an illustration of this point, McBride shared a story about what it takes to build a cathedral.

*People who created the plans to build a cathedral would create 200-year plans! They knew they would never physically step into the edifice that they were designing. Maybe their grandchildren or great-grandchildren would see the end result, but the designers and builders themselves would never walk into the building they were creating. What kind of mind does it take, and what type of practice and commitment does it take, to get up and work on something you know you will never see physically? To work every day with only a dream and imagination that perhaps the next generations will enjoy what you've created. This is the type of work of belonging. My presence today is the gift of the decisions of a powerful Black woman three generations ago who survived slavery of the South as she dreamt of me. What are we working on and toiling over that won't be completed in our lifetime? That's when we know we're actually working on something. We need to influence the culture makers, the thinkers, the practitioners, the entrepreneurs, to build differently.*

# 5

# *Care*

*And one of the great problems of history is that the con-
cepts of love and power have usually been contrasted as
opposites, polar opposites, so that love is identified with a
resignation of power, and power with the denial of love . . .
What is needed is a realization that power without love
is reckless and abusive, and that love without power is
sentimental and anemic. Power at its best is love imple-
menting the demands of justice, and justice at its best is
power correcting everything that stands against love . . .
It is precisely this collision of immoral power with powerless
morality which constitutes the major crisis of our times.*

MARTIN LUTHER KING, JR.,
last presidential address to the Southern Christian
Leadership Conference, August, 16, 1967

Mika is quiet most of the time when she's at home in her Brooklyn apartment. She isn't shy; she just prefers to listen to conversations, take long naps, and daydream to soft music. Her
hazel eyes are attentive and calming, and she has a way of making

you feel at ease when she greets you. From time to time she enjoys taking walks in the nearby park with the only person that understands her, her best friend, confidant, Alex. The first time I met Mika was by Zoom video conference, and I could feel her sincerity and warmth through my computer screen when she smiled at me and jumped into Alex's lap. Mika stared directly into his eyes and kissed him—well, she actually licked him. It's the only way she greets Alex. Mika is about fifty years old in human years, but in dog years she's only about ten. To Alex, Mika is not just a loyal, red nose pit bull terrier, nor just a pet to keep him entertained. No, Mika is a guide and a teacher that saved his life and led him through a tumultuous journey from violence to compassion, nurturing, and care.

Alex introduced Mika to me as his companion and proudly described how he and Mika had been together for nearly ten years. "She's part of my journey," Alex explained. Alex is in his early twenties and grew up on the streets of Brooklyn, New York. He is soft spoken, gentle, and his youthful eyes have seen more than most people his age. His deep New York accent blended perfectly with his gray hoodie and his neatly conditioned cornrow braids that his friend had just completed. Alex speaks with eyes first; then after a few seconds of thought, contemplation, and reflection, he responds with soft clarity and compassion.

Alex's mother purchased Mika as a Christmas gift. She didn't have much money to buy gifts because she used most of the money she earned from her job to support her crack cocaine addiction. But Christmas of 2010, she wanted to get something special for her son. She remembered from her last visit to the nearby apartment complex where she bought her drugs that the dog had just delivered a litter of puppies! The owner had bred his pit bull terrier and was selling the puppies along with little bags of hard, brownish-white nuggets of crack. During a blustery chilly December afternoon, she walked around the corner to the apartment to inquire about buying a puppy for her son, which would be a perfect gift. When she arrived, the owner gave her a price for each of the healthy puppies, but it was more than she could afford. But there was one that was really small, quiet, and from the looks of it, a little sick. Mika was the runt of the litter, and the owner sold the puppy to Alex's mother for fifteen bucks. She paid for the puppy and brought the little runt home to Alex.

Alex was excited when he first met the puppy, but Mika was terrified. During the first month, she would urinate when she was afraid of something and run to hide from everything except Alex. There was something about Alex's demeanor that comforted Mika and made her feel safe in her strange new apartment with a long dark hallway and the unfamiliar smell of corn bread and Raid bug spray. Alex didn't know anything about raising a puppy, or taking care of any pet for that matter, because he had never had one. Initially, he didn't understand why Mika was afraid of everything, he didn't know when she needed to be taken out for a walk, and he hated when she would go to the bathroom in his room. So he did what he thought was best: disciplined her and put her in a cage that someone had given him. Initially, he didn't understand Mika's needs, and she didn't understand his. But somehow, over the years, nestled between walks in the park and long talks about life on the couch, Mika changed Alex. She showed him how to nurture, be patient, and have compassion. Most of all, Mika, the ten-year-old red nose terrier, had taught Alex the most important lesson of his life, to love and to care about himself.

## TRANSFORMATIVE RELATIONSHIPS

Most of us, if we're lucky, have someone or something we care about. We care for our children with precious attentive nurturing, we care for our spouse or partner with unconditional and selfless support, we care for our pets as our best friends and important members of our families. Care is one of those things that we sometimes take for granted in our relationships. But where do we learn to care? Is care something that we can learn? Why is care important for our movements for justice and healing? In our pivot toward a healing-centered society, care is perhaps one of the most important ingredients to cultivate transformative relationships.

Mika didn't know, of course, that she had created a transformative relationship with Alex. Mika needed Alex to feed her, provide comfort and safety, and care for her needs. But it was the care that Mika needed that transformed Alex. Alex needed to become someone that he didn't know was possible. He had to discover something about himself, hidden deep inside, that he had never seen—compassion. Now, I know y'all are probably thinking, *really?* All this sounds a bit overly dramatic; all Alex needed to do was to take care of a dog. But Alex never learned care from his momma or compassion from his friends. Growing up on the streets of Brooklyn can be unforgiving, and a tough place to learn about vulnerability, compassion, and care. Most of Alex's life, until he met Mika, was filled with transactional relationships.

While relationships are complex, there are generally only two types that we have in our lives, *transactional* and *transformative*. We all are familiar with transactional relationships because they are everywhere. Transactional relationships are based on the performance of roles and the execution of tasks. Most of the time, transactional relationships are defined by the titles of our jobs or occupations. Transactional relationships are efficient in that they quickly help define how we engage with each other. Take for instance your trip to the grocery store or farmers market. You choose your items and take them to the register to determine the amount you need to pay. The cashier performs the task, you provide the cashier with the money in exchange for your items, and you both move on with your day. Now, there is nothing wrong with transactional relationships. Without this sort of relationship, it would be difficult to do our jobs. Transactional relationships help us get things done quickly without having to figure out how to engage with all the roles we play at work, at home, or in our communities. The challenge is that when our society is dominated by transactional relationships, and our systems are governed by performing tasks, and our daily interactions are based on efficiency, we slowly begin to erode our capacity for care, compassion, and all the things that make us human.

Transformative relationships, on the other hand, are based in those features of life like care, vulnerability, love, curiosity, connection. Transformative relationships are formed when we exchange pieces of our humanity with each other. When we do that, we give permission to others to do the same. These types of relationships are formed when we invest our precious time, our sacred secrets, and our raw vulnerability into each other. Transformative relationships are not neat, clean, and efficient like transactional relationships. No, transformative relationships are messy, confusing, and time-consuming, but they are always worth it because they create deep connections between us, force us to see things about ourselves we hide from, and cultivate parts of ourselves that we didn't know were possible. Chances are that the transformative relationships you have in your life were created over time and endured a bumpy road along the way. There comes a time in these sorts of relationships when simply performing predefined roles (teacher and student, customer and cashier, coach and player, CEO and employee) is just not enough to get through troubled waters together. When that happens, and life shows up in unexpected ways, transactional relationships won't do. We need someone who will ride with us all the way to the end, even if there's no end in sight.

The first time I learned the power of transformative relationships was the birth of my son, Takai. I remember bringing him home wrapped in a thin white hospital blanket with blue and pink stripes. My wife and I were so excited, and all we could think about was finally settling into our new family. But there are so many things they don't tell you about starting a family, like colic—the intense prolonged crying, inconsolable screaming, and persistent discomfort a baby experiences. The first couple of weeks we thought the colic would just pass, but it didn't. For six months, we listened to doctors, grandmothers, parents, and friends explain to us why our baby boy had colic and precisely what we needed to do to treat it. In fact, the only thing more frustrating than the colic was people giving us advice on what to do about it. We tried everything from placing warm towels on his belly to changing my wife's diet, laying him on his stomach, burping him three times after feeding and three times before bed, and late-night car rides to get him to sleep. But nothing we tried worked. By the fifth month, we were sleep deprived, exhausted, irritable, and, well, it wasn't good. Then suddenly, something changed. Not with my son's colic, but with me.

I reached out to a mentor, "Q," who has always provided me guidance and advice. Q is short for Afrie Quamina. He is tall, and I suppose during his younger years he probably sported an Afro, but now he is bald. His thick mustache always complements the colors of the dashiki he wears. Talking to Q is a bit like chatting with Yoda from *Star Wars*. He smiles with his eyes as if he knows the answer, before you even know you have a question. I suppose some people would call Q a mystic because he always knew the root cause of what you thought was the real problem. Oftentimes, my discussions with him would meander into long, seemingly tangential stories, veer off into cosmic confusion, and somehow, someway, he would land our convoluted conversation precisely on the very point that I needed to hear. I called Q for advice about what to do about my son's colic. I told him everything that my wife and I were dealing with, how the colic had not subsided, and the exhaustion we were experiencing. He listened to me rant about all the techniques we had tried to treat the colic. He listened to my frustration about our sleep-deprived relationship, and he heard me complain about the stress of feeling unable to help my baby boy.

Most of the time, Q would share with me a seemingly irrelevant story. But this time, he went straight to the point and head-on to my problem. "Your problem is Shawn." He paused, and I waited for his wise profound answer about what I needed to do to deal with the colic. "You think you have a problem that needs to be solved." *Wait, what the hell is that, Q?* I thought to myself. *I need advice!* He explained that we have a tendency, particularly Black men, to want to solve problems before we even understand what the problem is. "Your son's colic has a purpose, and the purpose is to bring you and your wife closer together, to transform both of you so that your union remains compassionately intact. There is nothing for you to do about the colic, nothing for you to fix about your son, he's perfectly fine. The only thing that you need to work on is accepting what is happening, and let go of trying to fix it."

I exhaled, because his words felt like he had lifted a ton of bricks from me. I felt all the pressure, expectation, perceived incompetence, and failure immediately wash away from me in that instant. My relationship with my son didn't begin with me teaching him how to throw a ball or tie his shoe. Nope, our relationship began with him teaching me how to accept him as perfect. My relationship with my wife also transformed. I told Nedra about my conversation with Q, and we talked about how we were secretly blaming each other for our son's condition. Our secret blaming had created mounting resentment we tried to hide from each other. This dynamic also melted away. So instead of focusing on fixing colic, we just buckled up, helped Takai when his tummy hurt, and laughed our way through the journey. We had transformed!

I suppose this is what happened to Alex when he realized that Mika's life depended on him, that he alone was responsible for Mika. For the first time in his life, Alex didn't have the burden and pressure to be hard, uncaring, and ruthless. The streets required him to be that way, but Mika didn't. Mika just wanted to be safe, nurtured, and cared for, and that's what he did. Alex made mistakes, but Mika didn't judge him or try to fix him, and together they embarked on a journey that saved both of them.

## CLEAN

When Alex was eleven years old, he saw his older sister get punched in the face by a grown man. He hit her hard, and Alex could hear the crack of the man's big fist break his sister's delicate face. She fell to the ground, and the man just walked slowly away as if nothing had happened. At first Alex was angry, and then he just went numb inside. For a while, he just stood there, unsure of what to do with all that he was feeling inside. I mean, what could he do? He was only eleven and surely if the man didn't think twice about hitting his sister, he certainly would punch an eleven-year-old kid. It was in that moment that Alex told himself that to survive the hardcore reality of the streets, he had to also be hardcore, tough, and uncaring. So that's exactly what he did. The next seven years of his adolescent life were spent on the streets. Where his crew went, he followed, because he felt like he needed them. But eventually, like most young people forced into the streets for protection, Alex found himself on probation, living in group homes within the foster care system, and frequently going AWOL (absent without leave) so that he could be home with his mother.

His mother was a custodian, and she always kept the house clean. She taught Alex and his siblings how to clean, and her drug addiction didn't get in the way of her keeping her home tidy and clean. You could always tell when she was using drugs because the house would be really clean. Alex just wanted his mom to stay clean but didn't know how to support her.

There's something about not caring about anyone, or anything, that over time takes a toll on your soul. For Alex, the fighting, robbing people, stealing, selling drugs always felt empty, as if there was something missing. "I felt like I was glorifying something that I really wasn't. I was really trying to like, be someone I wasn't. It takes a lot of work to not care, to pretend like you don't give a fuck that you've shot someone, or taken the life of someone's son or daughter. It wears and grinds on your conscience to show people only the most ruthless part of you." But that is all Alex knew how to do. His family didn't talk much about their emotions, and even after he witnessed his sister getting punched in the face, no one really talked about it. They just stuffed it down and kept it moving. His crew only talked about fighting, popping someone, or disrespecting a woman. Not much room to share what's really going on deep inside.

The thick armor he wore to protect him from caring became really heavy for Alex, and it became his own personal prison.

*I felt like I was lost and I wanted friendship. I wanted to be around people that I could communicate with. But I've never really communicated to folks in my crew like that. We would just*

*always talk about killing somebody, rolling up to somebody's*
*hood to fight, selling drugs, always putting our lives on the line.*
*But I couldn't tell them, "Yo man, my mom on crack" . . . and*
*that shit don't feel right! I felt like what I really wanted was*
*definitely brothership, and I'm not even sure what that was, but*
*I wanted to be around people who care about me, and I want to*
*care about people too.*

Regardless of what you do for a living, your race, age, or gender, or where you are reading this book right now, chances are that you have felt a little like Alex at some point in your life. There may be times when you need to connect with someone and share good news or something troubling. Sometimes we don't need advice as much as we just need to be heard, seen, and cared for. Eventually, Alex had a choice to make: either continue the transactional and destructive relationships he had with his crew, or explore the transformative relationships that were being cultivated in a local nonprofit organization that was training him to be an organizer in his neighborhood. At first, Alex thought he could do both—he would learn how to become a community organizer and sell drugs at the same time. Despite the fact that he and his crew lived together, they really didn't know each other. But things came to a head when Alex's mentor, Ricky, was released from prison. Ricky walked with a cane because he had cancer that made it hard to get around. Alex wanted to spend as much time with his friend as he could. During a warm summer afternoon, Ricky was returning to his apartment, walking slowly, leaning most of his weight to the right side where the cane would brace him. Someone stopped Ricky, exchanged a few words, and beat him badly, right there in front of his redbrick apartment building. Within an hour, Alex heard that Ricky had been beat up by someone in his own family. "They beat him up because they thought he was gay." Alex couldn't believe that someone could have so much hate in their heart for Ricky. So what if he was gay? Ricky had a heart of gold. Unfortunately, Ricky didn't survive the attack, as his injuries were so critical that he was unable to recover, and he died within a matter of months. Despite the fact that Ricky had family and friends in the neighborhood, very few came to his funeral. That's when things started to change for Alex. He began to wrestle with the fact that he was selling drugs and his mother was an addict, that no one trusted anyone in the neighborhood, and that no one seemed to care about anything. So after several similar altercations, Alex had had enough. He decided to leave the crew entirely.

At first, he didn't know what to do with himself. Alex had been selling drugs and hanging out with the same type of people for so long that he was unsure of how to change. But one day, instead of picking up his trap bag, he chose to focus his energy on caring for Mika. The first thing he did was get rid of the cage he kept her in most of the day. He remembered watching YouTube videos that said it wasn't good to keep dogs in a cage most of the day. He also bought a leash, and once or twice a day they would walk to the nearby park. When they returned home, they would sit and watch TV, and over time he realized that he needed her just as much as she needed him. Whenever he walked into his apartment, Mika would greet him with a warm trusting smile, and a hearty lick in the face!

## JUSTICE AND CARE IS LIKE PEANUT BUTTER AND JELLY

When we think about the term *care*, most of us conjure up images of parents caring for their children, or a nurse or doctor caring for a patient. We tend to think about care as an act of selfless support to one another, or the capacity to provide nurturing comfort and guidance, and there is plenty of research that confirms this. Take for instance researchers at Arizona State University who have studied the act of embracing.[1] Their data showed that when we embrace, our blood pressure lowers, there is a reduction in cortisol levels (a hormone related to stress), and an increase in oxytocin, which is also referred to as the cuddle or bonding hormone because it is released when people cuddle (hug) or bond socially. Other research illustrates that we have been hardwired to care, and we are neurologically wired to connect with others, because mirror neurons in our brains are stimulated when we're interacting with other people.[2] "Literally, when you are talking to someone, neuro-pathways in your brain light up to mirror the emotions and behaviors that this other person is conveying."[3] This is also what happens when babies are learning emotions and bonding with caregivers. Have you ever noticed that when you are looking in a baby's face and start smiling or cooing, they tend to reciprocate those same emotions back to you?

But care is also deeply rooted in our notions of justice and goes beyond a lens of a neuroscience. Our movements for justice are fundamentally about how we collectively have concern and empathy for one another. Care is our collective capacity to express concern and empathy for one another. It requires that we act in ways that protect, defend, and advance the dignity of all human beings, animals, and the environment. This gets at the core of what justice is about: the act of caring for the well-being and dignity of others. We've seen this so vividly in the global support of Black Lives Matter after the tragic death of George Floyd; we've also seen this in March for Our Lives following the tragic school shooting at Marjory Stoneman Douglas High School in Parkland, Florida. We cannot separate justice from caring—they go together just like peanut butter and jelly.

The power of care, however, is so underestimated in our efforts for justice. For the most part, our work for justice has become increasingly transactional, focusing on the tactical, strategic, and logistic areas of the work because it's easier than taking the time to really know folks. Care requires an emotional commitment and a psychic investment that take time, vulnerability, and deep concern for each other. I suppose that's why those of us who have experienced some form of alienation, rejection, or outright harm have empathy for those in similar situations. For instance, it's more likely that we understand the plight of our trans brothers and sisters when we've been harmed, rejected, or seen as disposable by larger society ourselves. All the rejection, alienation, exploitation actually creates a potion for deeper empathy across our differences.

Care is also the actions we take that say "You matter to me. What you think, how you feel, what is happening in your life is important to me, too." When we care, we participate in "humane investment," wherein we are able to sit, be with, and reflect on someone else's humanity. Transformative relationships are formed through this willingness to be still, to listen, and to share both our sorrows and our joys. When we exchange pieces of our humanity, become vulnerable, and begin to care and trust, it gives others permission to do the same.

Much of our thinking about care has been influenced by what we see on TV or social media. The term *self-care* for example has become popular among social justice advocates as a way to convey the need to take care of ourselves. Now, taking care of ourselves is important because we all work too much and often put everything and everyone before our own health and well-being. But the term *self-care* conveys this idea that caring for yourself is a sort of privilege and a good thing to do when you have the time and money. We call it "self-care," separating it from "normal care," because most of the time care is considered to be something we do for others, not for ourselves. Picture yourself going away to a yoga resort, spa weekend, or meditation retreat. Or maybe just coming home from work and taking a long bath with candles without disruption from the kids. These images of self-care are self-indulgent escapes where we tell ourselves not to feel guilty because we deserve it and have earned the privilege to escape for a while.

When we think about care in this way, it's basically akin to saying, "My well-being isn't dependent upon yours." The term *self-care*, while important, reinforces the idea that we are separate, disconnected, and independent from one another. We know from the COVID-19 pandemic of 2020 that our well-being is deeply interconnected and that if one of us is sick, we all are at risk. This is why I use the term *collective care*, not to discount the value of your massage, warm bath, or quiet walk in the park, but rather to cultivate an awareness that caring for ourselves is deeply connected to the well-being and concern of others. This is fundamentally what our movements for justice are based on, and there are no movements without shared concern and care for others.

Care, when viewed collectively and holistically, has three levels. The first level is *individual care*, where care focuses on concern for self. This is like the self-care where we do things, for the most part, to assure that we are OK. Individual-level care is a result of individualism and the notion that we are separate from others. At the individual level, care is about the preservation of one's own desires and is focused on what one wants to do. Generally, individual-level care has little to do with the concerns of others, but rather it aims to protect oneself from harm and being hurt. I wouldn't say individual care is just selfish indulgence because, from time to time, we all need to focus on caring for ourselves. The danger with individual-level care is that it sometimes fails to connect self-care to the concerns of others. It means that when we focus on our own care, we also have to ensure that we understand its impact on others. For example, when Alex decided to leave his crew, he made the choice because he wanted to exercise the capacity to care for others by caring for himself. He shifted his focus to caring for Mika, an example of care as interdependent. In our movements, and our daily life, we haven't built in much space for individual-level care.

Beyond the individual level, we need to cultivate the awareness of how our well-being is interconnected, which is the second level of care, *interpersonal care*. The interpersonal level focuses on the care we take in our relationships with others. At this level there is a strong emphasis on ethics of care like responsibility, commitment, and selflessness, all of which contribute to transformative relationships. Interpersonal care is another way to describe how Native Indigenous people, Maori, and African nations practice care by focusing on the quality of interconnected relationships. In a review of literature on care among these ethnic groups, I found that interpersonal care—the idea that well-being is based in the quality of relationships and mutual concern for others—is seen as a buffer that protects individuals within the group as well as the broader community. Take for instance the term *cousin* or *kinfolk* in the African American tradition. On the surface these terms identify familial relationships between people. But we also use these terms to describe close relationships with one another that are not bound by family lineage. We have play cousins, or we might refer to someone as Auntie Jackie when Jackie is really your momma's best friend and not related to you by marriage or blood. This type of interpersonal-level care is based in culture norms, and it means that I care for your well-being as if you are my family.

The South African term *ubuntu* probably most closely describes interpersonal-level care. *Ubuntu* has been used throughout sub-Saharan Africa in various forms and means that humanness is found through our interdependence, collective engagement, and service to others. It means that the very concept of what it means to be human is viewed as our connection, care, and concern for other people. Ubuntu was popularized by Bishop Desmond Tutu in 1999 when he wrote in his book:

> *Ubuntu is difficult to render in a Western language. It speaks to the very essence of being human. When you want to give high praise to someone we say, "Yu, u Nobuntu"; he or she has Ubuntu. This means that they are generous, hospitable, friendly, caring and compassionate . . . it means that my humanity is caught up, is inextricably bound up in theirs . . . I am human because I belong, I participate, I share.*[4]

Interpersonal care, just like ubuntu, is found in our relationships with others and shaped by our efforts to sustain quality transformative relationships. Similar to ubuntu, the Mayan term *In Lak'ech* conveys the deep interdependence that comes from interpersonal care and means "you are my other me." Think about the level of interdependence to see someone as "my other me." How would you treat your other you? How would you care for your other you? Interpersonal care can also be seen in the Tagalog term *Isang basak*, which means "one fall" or "one clap." In Pinoy culture, this conveys the idea that if one falls, we all fall, and that the collective-unity clap conveys solidarity and collective caring.

The third level of care is *institutional care*, which is like a social contract that assures the well-being of everyone in the institution or society. This third level of care is forged by both values and rules that focus on the collective good rather than individual rights. Sometimes these are laws, other times these are rules and policies that are the results of movements for justice. Take for instance how institutional care and the concept of ubuntu provided the moral compass of South Africa's new constitution and drove the activities and deliberations of the country's Truth and Reconciliation Commission (TRC), which was responsible for ushering in an unprecedented national healing process. The TRC served as a bridge between healing South Africa's old wounds and creating a hopeful new future. In fact, the constitution states that "there is a need for understanding but not for vengeance, a need for reparation but not for retaliation, a need for ubuntu but not for victimization."[5] Similarly, the idea of institutional care can also be seen in New Zealand's 2019 well-being budget. Moving beyond gross domestic product, the government focused on structuring the national budget to prioritize and assure the well-being of New Zealand citizens. The budget focused on new resources for mental health, child poverty, and job training for a new economy, just to name a few priorities.

## HOW WE LEARN TO CARE

After a speech I gave about the importance of care at a conference some years ago, a couple of bright graduate students came up and asked me if care was something that can be taught or can they be trained to care. At first, I was taken by surprise by their questions. During my talk, I was only concerned that people recognize the importance of caring relationships with young people and had never really thought much about how to teach or train people how to care. I'm not sure I really answered their question, because at the time I really didn't have a good answer. But since that time, I've come to realize a few things about how we learn to care and form transformative relationships.

First, we are all born with empathy and the capacity to care for each other. The trick is, we are socialized in ways that move us away from caring. Alex didn't really have to learn to care for Mika; it was already in him. He just needed the right conditions to allow himself to care. He didn't need to take an online course that trained him to care for Mika; he found himself caring for her because his surroundings and choice to focus on something else provided him with the opportunity to care in ways that he didn't know were possible. The same is true for us. We don't need to learn to care or be trained to have empathy for one another; we are wired to care and it's already in us. Even though the ability to care exists within every person, we need the right conditions and opportunities to practice and exercise this muscle. Unfortunately, the work environment may not be one of those places, as our jobs sometimes only reward transactional relationships. That's why it is so hard to practice caring at work—the conditions aren't right, so we remain transactional.

Second, if we are born to care and hardwired for empathy, we need to make space for it in our daily lives and in our work lives. I know, you might be saying, "There is no way I feel safe enough at work to form caring relationships. All that matters at my job is output and performance." But a few small things can make a huge difference over time. For example, at the beginning of your next staff meeting, rather than jumping directly into the agenda, start with an emotional check-in. This is a simple way to hear how people are feeling and to convey that how they feel matters. Another simple way to create the conditions for care might involve having the leader of the institution share their personal journey. Not their professional journey, but the personal stuff that requires some vulnerability. Doing these things over time creates the safety necessary for truly transformative relationships. Once you have done this, notice how your attitude and feelings toward the work you are doing change as you move from transactional interactions to transformative and human interactions. Similarly, we can sometimes get in the rut of routines at home with family. These routines can create the conditions for transactional relationships even with people close to us.

Cook dinner, do the dishes, check the kids' homework, take the kids to soccer, and repeat. But when we make space to ask our family members how their day went and what support they need in that moment to carry out their chores, a transactional task can turn into a transformative interaction.

Third, in order to build more empathetic movements, and for us to be grounded in healing-centered leadership, we have to practice caring as an act of courage. Care in the sense of human concern is the one thing that has fueled movements for justice and the only thing that can continue to push us forward to create the type of society we want to see. But it takes work. We have to take care of ourselves as an act of power, and value how our collective and interconnected work can both protect and heal.

# 6

# *Vulnerability*

*You have to be hurt . . .*
*And go through a lotta changes to sing the blues.*

BOBBY "BLUE" BLAND

My uncle Kenny was a blues man. He didn't just listen to blues music, he walked, wore, and savored every delicious corn-battered, deep-fried nugget that only Muddy Waters, Bobby "Blue" Bland, or B. B. King could offer. Uncle Kenny reminds me of a classic version of the late comedian Bernie Mac. Yeah, if you can picture Bernie Mac in his impeccable suits, polished shoes, and full Blackman swagger, you know he learned it from my uncle Kenny. Uncle Kenny was tall and dark, and when he smiled his white teeth stood in stark contrast to his beautiful, deep, dark-bluish black skin. When he laughed, he didn't hold back and laughed from his gut, loud and rolling as if he wanted everyone to feel the humor. His laugh was contagious and would fill up a large room. I don't recall when Uncle Kenny introduced me to the blues, but I know that I've always admired his passion for the music. "Blues is about life, the good and the bad," he would say, but I didn't come to appreciate the art until later in my life. His favorite song was "Stormy Monday" by Bobby "Blue" Bland. Now, you might not have ever listened to the blues, or you might not even like the blues, but there is something deeply honest, soulful, and vulnerable about each line of that song.

*They call it stormy Monday. . . .*
*But Tuesday's just as bad.*
*Wednesday's worse and Thursday's awww so sad.*

The blues was created from the beautiful struggle and born from vulnerability. It's about the soul opening up and pouring out whatever is in it without shame, blame, or polish. When done well, the blues is raw, gutbucket truth-telling, but to get there requires vulnerability and courage. It must be tough to write and sing the blues. The artist has to dive headfirst into some emotional murky waters—some real honesty about stuff that's been rattling around deep inside—and put it all on display. The power of the blues is found in its ability to connect to parts of ourselves that we are afraid of, and it reminds us that we are all human, struggling desperately and trying our best. It may seem odd to say that there is power in our vulnerability, and that our capacity to share parts of ourselves, even the parts we hide from, gives us enormous strength. But most of the time, we avoid vulnerability because it takes hard emotional work. It's not easy to tell the world you're broke, your woman has left you, and your dog and best friend just died. But when we are vulnerable, we find a sense of power and freedom. At least, that's what I feel like when I hear the blues.

Vulnerability is emotional risk taking, putting it on the table, and trusting that you won't be hurt when you do. Vulnerability is also the only way to form true transformative relationships because it raises the emotional stakes and creates a sacred agreement that what you just shared will be held and protected with tender care, without judgment. Vulnerability builds trust and creates emotional bonds that matter. Vulnerability is just like the blues: you speak your truth and put it out there so you can heal and continue on your way. Just saying it sometimes makes the load lighter.

Now, I know most of us are scared as hell of vulnerability because there are times when we've been hurt, ridiculed, and shamed after sharing something close to our hearts. But we also have to be careful about who we share our vulnerability with. We can't just go around spilling our guts to everyone. Brené Brown says in her work on vulnerability and shame:

> *Our stories are not meant for everyone. Hearing them is a privilege, and we should always ask ourselves this before we share: "Who has earned the right to hear my story?" If we have one or two people in our lives who can sit with us and hold space for our shame stories, and love us for our strengths and struggles, we are incredibly lucky. If we have a friend, or small group of friends, or family who embraces our imperfections, vulnerabilities, and power, and fills us with a sense of belonging, we are incredibly lucky.*[1]

## BLACK MEN AND VULNERABILITY?

Uncle Kenny was from Texas, and like my father he never really shared his emotions with me. Like most Black men, I really never learned to be vulnerable. My uncle Kenny and my father were forged from the idea that vulnerability was weakness, and men didn't have time to feel and share what was in their heart. But when I dig deeper, I realize that vulnerability looks and sounds different among Black men. Vulnerability is not just emotional disclosure and risk taking. For us, vulnerability is being there for each other when things get really hard, or just listening to each other over a beer. When Black men are vulnerable with each other and truly sharing our emotions, it might be disguised as laughing at a good joke, pauses of silence, or a tender response like "I really feel you, man." Our vulnerability is also rightfully guarded and protected because we have to survive racism and white supremacy, and sometimes it's just reinforced by paternalistic toxic masculinity. Truth is, however, I've seen Black men love, laugh, hug, embrace, and cry with one another, all over a cold Budweiser and a nice Hennessy. Vulnerability does exist among us Black men, but you have to earn the right to hear it.

Most of the time, though, we don't think about Black men as vulnerable. Black men in the United States have historically been positioned as both victim and victimizer. Common tropes of Black men as strong, nonfeeling, and hypersexualized served as a justification for enslavement necessary to support and grow the antebellum economy. Pseudoscientific and religious myths established a view of Black masculinity that both exploited Black men's physiology (physical strength, endurance, virility) and at the same time reinforced the notion that Black men were inherently violent and suitable for heavy, laborious work.

Unfortunately, today's social science research in many ways reinforces many of the same ideas about Black men. Just Google "black men research" and you'll find all sorts of articles about Black men's incarceration, fatal police encounters, health problems, and poor educational outcomes. Now, all of this research is important, but much of it focuses on the challenges Black men face in society. On one end of the spectrum of research are representations of Black masculinity as moral weakness. Unable to control sexual urges, emotions, and self-discipline, these are morally weak forms of Black masculinity. On the other end of the continuum are forms of research that focus on violence, aggression, privilege, and dominance. Both views leave us with a flat, one-dimensional view of Black men. Very little of this research has asked questions about ways that Black men experience vulnerability. The mosaics of experiences and textured realities of Black men's lives are rich and complicated with vulnerability—we just have to know precisely where to look. There are spaces of refuge, which are often hidden from public view, that allow Black men's vulnerability, and for moments at a time, we can confront and heal from the psychic wounds of the world.

For example, I've stopped watching YouTube clips of unmitigated police violence on Black unarmed residents in Black communities. I'll read about it online, but I won't click the blue hyperlink that takes you to the actual video. It's too painful and upsetting for me to watch because when I click the link, seeing the slightly blurry footage of complete disregard for another human being, a Black man or woman, makes me sick. I feel rage and sadness, rage, anger, rage, confusion, oh yeah did I say rage? Most of all, what's worse is that once the video of the gruesome ordeal is over, my first thought is that there will be another. I hate that I have to say that, but the truth is that there is a long way to go to heal the racialized dehumanization in our country.

The summer of 2020 was particularly tough for me and I suppose everyone else. My twenty-three-year-old son had come home from Los Angeles to be close to us during California's shelter-in-place orders due to the COVID-19 pandemic. You all remember my colicky infant—well, now he's twenty-three! Then it happened, news reports of Mr. George Floyd begging for his life as a white officer jammed his knee into Mr. Floyd's neck. I violated my rule this time, for some reason: I clicked the link and saw the ordeal for myself, and it changed me, and probably you as well. My eyes swelled up and I cried. Not so much from sadness, but the rage and anger that this actually happened. I watched it again, this time with my twenty-three-year-old son, and we sat quietly at our black kitchen table. We both inhaled and exhaled, and then he walked back into his room. No words were exchanged.

I wanted to ask him how he felt about what he had seen and if he wanted to talk about what was going on. I wanted to see if I could offer some good advice to my son. But he really didn't want to talk about it. Truth is, it was me that was worried about him. Did I raise him to hold on to his emotions? Was he insensitive to racialized trauma? Could he be the victim of the next police encounter?

About a week had passed when he decided that he was returning to Los Angeles. My wife and I agreed that it was way too soon for him to return, so we begged him to stay a little longer. There was so much happening out in the world. But he is a filmmaker and wanted to get back to his work. When it was time for him to leave, my wife and I said our goodbyes, and as he walked to his car, with his clothes sprawling from his duffel bag, I embraced him, and I prayed for his safety. I wanted to tell him to be safe, but he knew, as did I, that his safety was not entirely determined by him. He's Black, young, and six-foot-four, and police and people fear and hate him for that. They don't see him like I do. They don't know that his favorite childhood movie is *The Sandlot*, and that he loves rice and beans, or that his first word he uttered was "bubbles." So as we stood in our driveway, I embraced him with all my heart and held on for just a few seconds longer, and we prayed. We could hear a squad of police cars speeding past, and we could smell fire burning in the hills nearby. I found myself having to fight back the tears, but it wasn't much of a fight. Our eyes met, and he could see that I was wrestling inside, and he knew exactly what my opponent was. So he just returned an embrace. "I'm good, Dad, I'll be alright, don't worry. I love you." Then all was right with me when he said that. We smiled, and he threw his bag in the back seat, and we watched him drive slowly away, back to LA.

That moment of vulnerability helped me. We both knew, without really saying it, that we were concerned about—or, to be honest, afraid of—the profound uncertainty of the moment. I could be wrong, but that moment was a turning point in our relationship. I get the sense that even though he is in LA and we are in Oakland, we are closer. We simply don't take our being together for granted, and that matters in how we show up for each other.

## I CAN SEE YOU NOW!

I suspect that is the purpose of vulnerability in our relationships with others: to not take each other for granted and to show up in ways that matter. Vulnerability is like a portal to our humanity. When we open it up, what flows out is the beautiful mess and confusion that makes us human. When that happens, we can see each other more clearly, without the clutter of all the bullshit that we carry around. We use our titles, degrees, positions, and authority to determine how we show up and form relationships. But remember, when we interact with people based on our titles, we just reinforce transactional relationships. To form truly transformative relationships, we cannot skip vulnerability because it is the only way that we really see each other.

We need more transformative relationships in our lives, work, and institutions to create a healing-centered society. You probably already have transformative relationships in your life. These are the relationships where you both take emotional risks and share things that aren't neat, clean, and tidy about yourselves. I learned the power of vulnerability over the years of working with teachers, social workers, school principals, and youth-development workers. When I began training folks how to better work with young people of color, I would use the typical youth-development theories and approaches that I had been trained in. But I also knew that there was something missing in how I was training people to connect with young people. I knew that the most important thing in working with young people and their families was the relationship you had with them.

One of the most courageous acts of vulnerability I've ever seen occurred during a retreat I led with fifty social justice and educational leaders from around the country in 2018. We had convened in a beautiful venue in Northern California that was nestled between majestic redwoods to the east and views of the Pacific Ocean to the west. We had gathered to deepen our understanding of healing and transformation in our work. The goal during my session was to explore how the power of vulnerability could be transformative in our collective work for justice.

During the session, I explained to the group the process of othering (assigning negative attributes to groups unlike your own) and belonging (the practice of cultivating the capacity to see the humanity in groups unlike our own) and its consequences for our collective effort for social change. I described that our real work as leaders, if we really want to create a healing-centered world, is to recognize how the process of othering leads to separation and ultimately dehumanization. I explained that we all need to find some way to embrace the humanity among those groups that we find most unlike us. To make the point stick, I asked them to imagine a group of people that they would really not want to spend a week with. I asked them to identify the race, class, gender, geography, style of dress, and language of the group they were imagining. Then I asked them to share the group they had identified. Some people said that spending a week with a white fraternity would be really difficult. Another said that it would be really hard to spend time with a group of young military-trained police officers. Then someone mentioned that she would really find it challenging to spend time with a group of white, evangelical Christian, Republican, Trump-supporting women.

I explained that our transformation is interwoven with our capacity to see the humanity in the group they had just identified—this is where our work is. I could tell I had immediately struck a nerve because everyone's hand shot up, ready to hurl razor-sharp questions at me in disagreement with my comment. I anticipated questions like, "How am I supposed to see the humanity in racist and sexist groups when they refuse to see me as human?" I could tell this lesson was going to be difficult for the group to swallow, and I could anticipate and feel the vehement pushback from the group.

Steven, an African American brotha in his midforties who had been quiet during the retreat, raised his hand. He wore a blue hat with embroidered letters "CAL," and for some reason I called on him first. He paused with a bit of trepidation, and I expected him to push back in disagreement. He said, "I've been sitting here listening to you explain othering and how we all at times 'other' groups in our work. I also heard folks share groups of people that they are most unlike and would hate to spend time with. It's hard to sit here and listen to what I'm hearing from folks. Like people say that they couldn't spend a week with Republicans, or evangelical Christians, or Trump supporters." He paused, and the room was silent because we could feel he was holding something heavy he wanted to share with us.

"Well, this is hard to say to this group, but . . . I'm a registered Republican, I'm an evangelical Christian, and I'm a Trump supporter." He exhaled, as if he had breathed out twenty pounds of concrete that landed on the floor directly in the center of the room for everyone to see. The group was shocked at what he had shared, and so was I. "I've been feeling like I don't belong at this retreat because of some of the comments I've heard, and . . ." He paused, and as he composed himself, nearly everyone's eyebrows were raised, with confusion and disdain on their face. Folks' hands shot up again, eager to respond to what he had just shared. He continued, "I came to this retreat because I needed to be with people who were learning how to heal. You see, I lost my brother a couple of weeks ago, and it's so hard . . . I haven't even buried him yet." He lowered his head, and his voice cracked with emotional intensity. He looked up at us, his eyes were wet, and he said, "I need to heal too, I haven't had the courage to even bury him." His soul was open, and it spilled out on all of us. Almost immediately everyone's raised hands went down as if a wave of unanticipated compassion swept over the room. Strangers who hadn't connected with Steven gently placed their hands on his back and offered their support. We could see him.

Steven's vulnerability transformed our group. Not because it was a big Kum Ba Ya moment—quite the contrary. His comments unleashed conversations among people in the group who felt the same way as he did at times. Others felt unsafe, and that his presence violated a sense of connectedness, security, and well-being they needed. Our conversation about othering and belonging got real, and it was no longer just a theoretical discussion. Steven sharing his vulnerability encouraged others to do the same and made it possible for us to have a series of difficult and uncomfortable conversations. While we did not all agree with one another, people did engage in ways where we could see each other in more humane ways.

But the important lesson here is that vulnerability requires the delicate balance between risk and safety. I know, you might be thinking, is it safe for BIPOC to be vulnerable with their white colleagues? Under what conditions should I be vulnerable with groups of people who don't know me? How might I be vulnerable with people who despise me because of my gender? Well, there is also a politics to vulnerability that we need to explore.

# THE POLITICS OF VULNERABILITY

Who is vulnerable, at risk, disposable, and dispensable is at the heart of the politics of vulnerability. Our identities matter, and safety about who we are vulnerable with and how vulnerability works is important. Should I be vulnerable with men who objectify me? Should I be vulnerable with whites who dehumanize me? How, where, and why is vulnerability important for justice? These questions are important for us to weave the connection to how vulnerability builds transformative relationships and allows us to show up in ways that transform our institutions and society.

In order to transform the institutions in our society, we also have to transform how we show up in these institutions. Vulnerability is one way that we can begin to go deeper in building the types of relationships and teams that matter at work and in our personal lives. But we also have to be careful about what we mean by the term *vulnerability*. Research on vulnerability has been gaining popularity in recent years, sparked largely by Brené Brown's work on the topic. Most researchers have viewed vulnerability as an emotional state of potential harm. Studies of vulnerability examined a range of disabling qualities and diminished capacities resulting from places of helplessness or shortcoming. Brown came along and completely changed the game by showing us the power that can come from discovering vulnerability in our personal and professional lives. But I'm also mindful that there is a politics of vulnerability: some of us can afford to be more vulnerable than others. Power, privilege, and security are all conditions that can impact who is vulnerable, the consequence of being vulnerable, and what we gain from being vulnerable in our relationships. So while Brown's work on vulnerability is groundbreaking, we can build on her ideas to understand how issues of race, gender identity, social class, and power all determine the consequences of our vulnerability.

To understand the politics of vulnerability, let's return to the blues. Blues music is an art form that has roots in the deep South and is born from spirituals and field songs created by enslaved

Africans. The music evolved from African spirituals, chants, work songs, and field hollers into revivalist hymns and folk music. At the heart of the blues are stories that convey suffering and joy, struggles and triumph, pain and pleasure. What makes the blues so powerful is that the artist can connect to the lyrics from some deep personal experience. So when B. B. King says, "The thrill is gone . . ." he's singing it from a lived experience, the pain of going through heartbreak and the joy of coming out on the other side. It's a type of emotional vulnerability. But the blues was also shaped by *structural vulnerability*, the laws, policies, and values that create oppression and suffering. The fact that the blues originated on Southern plantations in the nineteenth century is in itself an example of structural vulnerability. Structural vulnerability means that in our society some groups (racial, gendered, social class, religion) are likely to experience some form of social misery like poverty. Social misery is not just an individual experience but a collective one. Yet these two forms of vulnerability (structural and emotional) work together. Structural vulnerability—poverty, gender marginalization, racial oppression—fuels and produces collective emotional harm and shared psychological injury—the ingredients for emotional vulnerability.

Now, here is the point: in order to transform structural vulnerability, we need to tap into our emotional vulnerability. When we have the capacity and ability to share our emotional vulnerability in our collective experiences with racism, classism, sexism, and poverty, we build bonds between us based in empathy. It allows us to see each other across differences and conjures the power we need to show up in ways that transform our relationships. When we do this, it opens the possibility for imagining, creating, and recreating new systems, policies, and structures. That's why hearing someone being vulnerable moves us. Take Steven for instance. Through his emotional vulnerability of sharing about losing his brother, we could see and feel his courage. In that moment some of our rigid boundaries like our political party and religious differences melted away, leaving only the truth standing. His sharing about a significant loss in his life prompted me to connect with losses in my own.

We see the courage and feel the honesty in what was shared, just like when we are moved by the blues; you can feel the truth deep inside, and this is true for any genre of music. When we can learn how to use vulnerability as a tool to convey our experience with suffering and joy, troubles and triumphs, that's when we are learning how to cultivate transformative relationships that matter.

## WADING IN SHALLOW WATER

In 2020 I served as the chairman of the board for a foundation in California. Our board members were racially diverse, generally progressive, and came from rural communities and large urban areas. One of my goals was to support the CEO and board of directors with developing an affirmative statement about racial equality and how the foundation might focus on addressing racial inequality in the state. The board members for the most part agreed that we could be more explicit about racial inequality, yet we had not discussed our own perspectives on race, racism, and racial inequality in any real depth. Realizing this issue, the foundation staff pulled together a series of learning sessions on the topic from top experts in the field. These were the heavy hitters of research, theory, and policy related to race and racial inequality. We heard from john powell, Angela Glover Blackwell, Manuel Pastor, Alicia Garza, and Ibram X. Kendi. Our learning journey with them was largely focused on terms, concepts, and theories about race and racial inequality. We spent a great deal of time reading and discussing the reading's ideas and concepts as they might relate to philanthropy. It was a good start, but still I sensed something was missing in our journey and felt like we were wading in shallow and safe water.

Not long into our journey, we received a memo from the staff that called attention to the need for the foundation to be more explicit about race and to commit to being an anti-racist organization. The memo used terms like *white supremacy* and *anti-Black racism*, which raised serious concerns among some of the board members. For other board members, these terms were like a breath of fresh air and affirmed their long-standing commitment to racial justice. The question before the board was, "What does it mean to be explicit about race and racial inequality?" For some, it meant to use terms like *diversity* and *inclusion*; for others it meant to use terms like *white supremacy* and *anti-Black racism*. During one of our meetings it was clear that we were not going to reach consensus about the board's position, and the foundation's direction, in regards to race and structural racism. One board member commented, "I'm offended by the term *white supremacy*. It's a blanket statement about white people as a whole." Others replied, "These terms reflect my reality—and the reality of so many people of color in California."

The CEO reflected on our deliberation and concluded that the language in the memo needed to be revised and nuanced to reflect the complexity of the board's views. It was a tense and complicated discussion because we didn't really have all the tools we needed to engage in real discussions about racial inequality. Even though our conversations were respectful, I could feel people's emotional responses to others' comments. I was watching folks with raised eyebrows, dismissing smirks, and urgent gestures to be called on next to smash on what someone had just said. It was going down in the boardroom! But I realized that the tools we were most familiar with were theoretical concepts, technical terms, and data about racial inequality. These tools are necessary, but they're insufficient when you need to go deeper into transformative change. I realized that the real problem wasn't opposing and unreconcilable views on race and racism; the real problem was that we didn't have a way to see each other's views and build consensus from our awareness of each other.

We decided that we needed more time on these issues; we needed to get underneath our views by hearing the stories that fueled them. So we planned the next board meeting for this purpose. When we met, we went through the technical aspects of the agenda like always. But we had allocated a few hours later in the day to be guided by a facilitator and sit with one another to hear our stories. We had been asked to bring an item (photograph, necklace, book, postcard) that represented who you are and where you are from. During this segment of our meeting, we didn't sit behind the boardroom table but rather in chairs in a large circle, side-by-side. The facilitator was masterful and explained to us that our stories were powerful portals into our identities, and by simply sharing our stories we were using the power of vulnerability. He began by playing an African drum and explained that the drum was used to call people together, celebrate, and heal. He had placed in the center of our circle a large red cloth highlighted with brown and black African symbols. By now we all knew that this wasn't going to be a typical discussion about race and racial inequality.

One by one, each person revealed the object they decided to bring and explained why they brought the object and what it revealed about their own story. I chose to bring an antique pocket watch that my aunt had given to me. It was my grandfather's old watch. On the back is etched "Homus Ginwright 1832," the name of my great-grandfather. So when it was my turn to share, I told the story of my father and how he learned to work with his hands. He could build and fix just about anything because my grandfather had taught him. I shared that my father would often tell me how, during the summer months in Florida, his father would clean the floors of wealthy white people who owned palatial beach homes. My father always dreamed that one day he could take his family back to stay in one of these homes, even just for the weekend.

During the next few hours, each person shared their story, and it was magical. I listened to people share childhood trauma, dreams of their immigrant parents, and lessons about life from the streets. Each story was vulnerable, honest, and pure, without the distraction of title, position, and status. As people shared their stories, they didn't hold back and were courageous. We all learned what it felt like to not fit in as a teenager, the experience of being humiliated for using food stamps, the shame of not being able to lose their accent, and the insecurity from being adopted. Most of all, we learned about each other in ways that allowed us to better understand our relative perspectives on race, as well as other topics. We enjoyed the gift of vulnerability, and we could see each other differently after that because we went deeper than abstract concepts and revealed our own stories about identity and where we came from. We were sharing, learning, and listening to our raw and gritty human stories; our board was playing the blues.

Vulnerability is not just something that we practice in our intimate relationships but something we need to make space for in our institutions as well. Most of the time, we just don't take the time to go deeper. But remember, vulnerability is the portal to transformative relationships. The only way we transform our relationships is by sharing pieces of our humanity with one another, in a safe space, and listening with our hearts. When we do that, we begin to see our stories in other people. We connect because vulnerability is like a sacred agreement to be present to someone else's humanity. Over time, when we connect like this, organizational culture will shift to deeper more meaningful connections among people.

Sitting in that circle together mattered in how we showed up for each other after that because we could see each other differently. So when the entire world joined and participated in #BlackLivesMatter in support of defending the humanity of Black people, our board unanimously supported the move with a 250-million-dollar allocation over ten years to support and advance Black-led organizing in California. My sense is that our decision wasn't simply out of social obligation, nor was it pressure to respond with a pithy "we support #BlackLivesMatter" statement that appeared on websites ranging from Starbucks to Target and even the NBA. The board's statement was born out of a deeper understanding of racial injustice and a more intimate understanding of each other. Going deeper using vulnerability as a guide paid off in the long run because even though we had disagreements about including rural poor whites, being more explicit about Latinx communities, and lifting up Native experiences, we could understand each other's true intent and deep motivation. That was made possible by vulnerability and a commitment to going to those places where our stories are born. When we learn to do that, we heal, see each other, and move together in the direction of justice.

# WHY VULNERABILITY MATTERS FOR JUSTICE AND HOW TO DO IT

In order to transform our movements and institutions, we need to cultivate transformative relationships among those who have common goals, and even among those with whom we disagree. Belonging, care, and vulnerability all provide the critical ingredients needed for us to pivot toward a more humane society. Researchers who study vulnerability generally understand the concept as a form of risk and exposure to threat. It's studied as something that should be carefully considered when thinking about groups of people who might be at risk from harmful social issues. For example, recent immigrants to the United States might be "vulnerable" to economic exploitation. Vulnerability in this sense is only structural and doesn't get to the deeper values that drive policies and institutional practices. This is entirely the type of vulnerability I'm referring to. I'm talking about vulnerability as a collective process of emotional disarming and communal risk taking with one another. Vulnerability in this sense requires both individual social-emotional reflection and institutional courage to make time and space for the journey.

In systems thinking, there is the concept that change occurs through multiple levels of a society or organization. I like the iceberg metaphor that I've seen used to describe this idea. At the top of the iceberg are events that we only react to. Just below the surface are patterns and trends that cause the events; usually we can anticipate these patterns. The next level down are underlying structures that give rise to patterns and trends. But at the deepest level are mental models, or deep assumptions, beliefs, and values that we hold about the world. These mental models are at the root of the underlying structures, which give rise to patterns and trends that create events.

In our movements and work toward justice we spend so much time responding to events, examining patterns, and sometimes changing the underlying structures, but very little time transforming our values, assumptions, and beliefs of how to show up in ways that allow us to play the blues together. We can only understand, and therefore transform, our deeper values and assumptions when we lean into vulnerability—share our stories, listen, and learn from one another. I know this isn't easy to do, particularly when there is so much toxic political difference that makes it hard to imagine how vulnerability would look in diverse political and racial settings. But these examples, while imperfect, provide us a glimpse into what vulnerability looks like in practice.

Take for instance the activities and deliberations of South Africa's Truth and Reconciliation Commission, which was responsible for ushering in an unprecedented national healing process. The Promotion of National Unity and Reconciliation Act of 1995 established the commission to expose the human rights violations that had existed in South Africa from 1960. The commission's purpose was to make full public disclosure of the human rights violations that occurred and grant amnesty to those who disclosed their participation. The commission also served as an opportunity for victims to openly share the violations they suffered. The only path toward national unity was through vulnerability, and for more than seven years, South African citizens shared their stories as perpetrators and victims of what they'd done or what had been done to them under apartheid. Their stories were broadcast around the country for everyone to see, and where no one could hide. The country was vulnerable, and while not perfect, the painful process helped heal the wounds of the past.

So what can you do to practice vulnerability in your work for justice? How can vulnerability help us pivot toward a more healing-centered society? I usually try to avoid cookie-cutter step-by-step recipes or how-to conversations about matters related to healing. It is not just what you do but really the intent behind why you do it. There are some questions and actions that you can use to lean into vulnerability in your work toward justice. For the most part, these questions and prompts encourage deeper thinking about what we are doing on a daily basis and why we are doing it. Ultimately, if we continue to practice these actions, we step more confidently into spaces of vulnerability that make a difference.

**Do I have transformative relationships with people in communities I care about?** Sometimes we engage in social change work from a distance and yet are close enough with people to practice vulnerability. Nearly every issue I care about—youth voice, racism, trauma, criminal justice—was born out of a transformative relationship with someone who taught me more than I thought I knew about the topic. This meant sitting in a circle with young Black men on probation listening to their stories, or spending time in a men's correctional facility and learning about compassion, or sitting at the kitchen table with mothers who were so stressed from daily doses of trauma. When we share our stories, we connect in ways that build bonds of understanding.

**Ask if it's safe to be vulnerable.** Building the container for vulnerability is just as important as vulnerability itself. It is important to assess if it's relatively safe enough to practice vulnerability. Now, this is tricky on the one hand because vulnerability, by its very nature, means social emotional risk taking. It means that there is something at stake when you share something that matters. On the other hand, if it is too safe, then there is no risk and therefore no growth in the relationship. The important thing to ask is, "Will or could I be harmed by sharing this?" If the answer is yes, then you should rethink participating. But if the container is cultivated correctly, you'll feel safe enough to share your story because you've already considered if the person or group has earned the right to hear your story.

**Create time and space, then repeat.** Vulnerability happens over time and with people you trust. As a leader, your job is to cultivate the time and space in your work to guide people back to their authentic stories. You might try having people share an artifact that represents their family history or draw their journey from childhood to now. And do it more than once, using different methods. Making space for people to share their stories in an intentional way creates the pivot we need in our movements and organizations.

We all have stories that can heal ourselves and our society; we just need the time and space to share them. So open up your favorite music app and listen to the blues for a while. You'll find, if you really listen, stories of raw vulnerability that can connect with your own story of joy, pleasure, sadness, and disappointment. These are the things that make us human, and if we make space enough in our lives to listen, we can find the real secret to our own transformation, which is of course the only real way we change the world.

## *Pivot 3*
# From Problem to Possibility

# 7

# *Perspective*

*I recently passed that marker of middle age and got bifo-
cals. . . . For three weeks I felt dizzy. I had trouble climbing stairs. Reading in bed gave me a headache. But then
my eyes learned; they transitioned seamlessly and saw
the whole. . . . We humans have the inherent capacity to
move between two seemingly diametrically opposed ways
of seeing, near or far, either/or, and make of them both/
and. I'd lost this ability, I'd regained it with new glasses,
and only now can I appreciate the miracle.*

ELIZABETH JARRETT ANDREW,
in *Queer Voices: Poetry, Prose, and Pride* edited by
Andrea Jenkins, John Medeiros, and Lisa Marie Brimmer

Malcolm's home is surrounded by tall, lush willow trees. In
fact, just about everyone in his neighborhood enjoys the semi-
privacy that the trees provide when they are relaxing in their
backyards. Malcolm noticed that Kisha, his neighbor directly behind
his home, was building something in her backyard. The trees blocked
his view, so he wasn't sure quite what she was building; all he saw

were ropes hanging from a structure. So he called Javier, who had a much better view of Kisha's backyard. "What is Kisha building in her backyard?" Malcolm asked.

Javier walked over to his fence and peeped through a hole that had been there for years. With his cell phone in one hand and a cold beer in the other, he replied, "She is building a deck. I can see it from the hole in my fence." But Malcolm wasn't convinced that she was building a deck—after all why would a deck have so many ropes?

So Malcolm called Vien, the neighbor on the other side of Kisha's house. He was sure that Vien could see what Kisha was building in her backyard. Vien peered through her fence, and to her surprise she saw what Kisha was building. Vien quickly reported back to Malcolm, "That gurl is building a small guest home, I can see it, she just put in a door."

Still not convinced, Malcolm walked to his back fence and peered over to see for himself. He was shocked at what he saw. "What the hell? Looks like she is building a boat, complete with an anchor and ropes."

Later that day, Malcolm, Javier, and Vien all met up at Starbucks to share notes about Kisha's backyard project; they loved to gossip about all the neighborhood shenanigans. But nothing they said made any sense. Javier swore she was building a deck and even described the redwood hand railing that was installed. Vien laughed at Javier's silly deck story and explained that Kisha was building a guest house; she even described the yellow front door. Now Malcolm was confused. Because when he pulled himself up over the fence, he could see the bow of a boat.

Each one of them quickly discounted each other's version of what they saw. Which really pissed off Javier. "I know what I saw, my friend. You don' t need to insult me with such bullshit about a guest house or a boat," Javier said, raising his voice.

Vien replied, "Wait, Javier, I know you drink a lot in the afternoon, are you sure you saw a deck?"

Malcolm quickly corrected Vien, "Both of y'all got it twisted, Kisha is building a damn boat."

Just when they had begun arguing, Kisha walked right into Star-bucks. They abruptly stopped arguing and had that guilty look on their faces, like they were talking about someone who just entered the room. Kisha didn't care though, so she walked over to them and blurted out, "I guess y'all wondering what I'm building in my backyard."

They stuck to their stories. Javier said, "I see you are building a deck." Vien replied, "I see you are building a guest house," and Mal-colm just said, "That boat you are building is nice."

Kisha knew they were all wrong and replied, "Y'all come by later this afternoon, and I'll show you all what I'm building. You won't believe it when you see it."

* * *

You probably recognize this story as the remix to the six men who are blind and the elephant. As the parable goes, six men who are without sight, having never seen an elephant, describe parts of the elephant from their relative perspective. One of them feels the trunk and claims that the elephant is like a long snake, while another grasps the tusks and concludes that an elephant is like a sharp spear, and still another man feels the elephant's large and rough leg and concludes that an elephant is a tree. Unable to see the entire animal, they assume that the others' descriptions are wrong and deceptive, and an argument ensues.

Most of us are a lot like Malcolm, Javier, and Vien—we peer through fences in our lives and conclude that what we see on the other side is the entire story. And just like the visually impaired men with the elephant, we all have limitations about what we see without an awareness of our limitations. We believe that *our* ver-sion of the world is *the* version of the world. This idea is easier to say than it is to put into practice because we need some assurance that our experience and interpretation of the world are based in fact and have meaning. How else would we confront racism when we see it? How would we address homophobic behavior at work? How would we know to call out sexist language among close friends or family?

Our perspective on these issues gives us insight into a world of how power and oppression work even if it's invisible to most people. It's our perspective that gives us the superpower to identify Islamophobia when others say, "She was just joking when she made that comment, she really didn't mean anything by it."

The truth is that sometimes we are not aware about how our perspective can shine light onto some things and obscure others. Sometimes we are just too close to see the whole thing; we have a limited view of what is really happening. Most of the time we don't question what we see; we just act on it as if it were true. When we make a pivot in our perspective, however, and become aware of the possibility that our perspective is limited, by stepping back we gain a fuller perspective on what we see. Gaining perspective is not a matter of being right or wrong, but rather it just means that we pull back and become curious about a possible bigger picture.

Not long ago my wife, Nedra, and my college-bound daughter, Nyah, were leaving our home to catch a flight back to Los Angeles. Nedra had decided that she needed to accompany her daughter to the airport to ensure that Nyah didn't miss the flight. At precisely 8:35 A.M., Nedra opened her Lyft app on her phone to request a driver to take them safely to the airport. As usual, they both were frantically packing up until the last moment before the Lyft driver arrived. They grabbed all the luggage and rolled it outside to the curb and waited for the driver to finally pull up. We have a modest home in Oakland, and from time to time, we place yard signs in our small front yard that say things like "In This House, We Believe No Human Is Illegal" or "#BlackLivesMatter" or "Kindness Is Everything," real San Francisco Bay Area progressive stuff. The Lyft driver arrived, and he was a white man in his early sixties, and most of his hair was white and gray. After Nedra and Nyah placed their luggage in his trunk, they jumped into the back seat. They noticed him reading the signs in our front yard. He didn't nod or smile, so Nedra greeted him with her normal bubbly and warm, "Hey, how are you doing today?" The driver didn't respond and simply pulled off as if she had not said hello. Nedra again said, "Hello, it's a nice morning, isn't it?" No response from the driver.

Now, some people can tolerate rudeness. They can see it and walk away without incident, but not Nedra, and by now Nedra knew that he was ignoring her for some reason. She concluded that he must be conservative based on his age and race. She thought to herself, *He saw all the progressive signs in our front yard and his stomach must be turning.* To make matters worse, she said to herself, *He is driving two Black women to the airport, his racism must be raging right now.* So Nedra asked him, "What do you think about the signs in our front yard?" Yet again, he didn't even turn his head to reply; he just kept driving without saying a word. Nedra was furious, and turned to my daughter, who was listening to music on her headphones. "Did you see that? Is he really ignoring me?"

My daughter put her headphones back on and calmly responded, "Mom, he didn't ignore you, he just didn't hear you." Then she pointed toward a small sign attached to the back seat of the car that read Driver Is Deaf.

Nedra had concluded, from her limited perspective, that the driver was ignoring her because his conservative views conflicted with ours. From where she was sitting, it might have been difficult to see the sign, or maybe she couldn't see the sign because her past experience with sexism, racism, and sixty-year-old white men ignoring her brilliance had already defined for her what was happening. But the truth was, the Lyft driver was deaf and could not hear her.

How much of our lives do we spend unaware of our perspectives? How often do we step back to see that our viewpoint is limited, not wrong or right, but simply obstructed? Sometimes our immediate response is to put up a wall and defend our own interpretations. Even when we step back to look at the bigger picture, we still hold on to our interpretations because our viewpoint is the only one possible. We just can't see the whole thing. A pivot in our perspective means that we become more aware of those things that obstruct and obscure how we see the world and act within it. We gain a more complete vantage point to understand what is happening around us and a greater capacity to respond in ways that are restorative, healing-centered. But first we have to learn to become an observer, the witness to all and other perspectives and viewpoints, without judgment but with curiosity. The pivot in perspective means that we actively work, even when it's hard as hell, to recognize that there is always a bird's-eye view of things that allows us to see the whole picture.

There is an important distinction between being "proximate" to something, in the sense that Bryan Stevenson reminds us of in his book *Just Mercy*, and gaining perspective. For Stevenson, getting proximate means getting closer to the issue you care about. He encourages folks to get to know the issue closer up, not just from the statistics in a report but from people's lived experiences and stories. It's true that sometimes we engage in justice work from a distance and are not close enough with people who are struggling with the issue.

Stevenson is really speaking to people who read about mass incarceration but have never spent time in a prison. He wants folks to have greater proximity to an issue because they gain deeper understanding, a clearer vantage point, when there is a personal connection. Similarly, for those of us who are working on issues like mass incarceration, women's rights, or voter engagement, we also have work to do—not being more proximate, but just the opposite. We gain a better perspective when we cultivate our capacity to see the bigger picture, the bird's-eye view.

Mr. George Floyd's murder in 2020 is akin to Mr. Emmett Till's murder in 1955. Both awakened the moral conscious of the world to act, rise up, and reclaim a Black humanity. There is something about bearing witness to the absolute disregard for human life that can sometimes cut through ideological differences. Now with perspective we can see the beautiful consequences of Mamie Till's decision to have an open casket. Perhaps with perspective we can understand what Dr. King meant when he said the long arch of history bends toward justice. Perspective, viewpoint, vantage all help us see the entire picture even when we are too close to see what's on the other side of the fence.

* * *

Malcolm, Javier, and Vien all descended on Kisha's driveway anticipating her big backyard reveal. She met them in the driveway with her new toy, a small red and black drone. "I just picked this up from Best Buy and I love it, and it's the best way to see what I'm building." So Kisha flicked on the power, and the drone came to life. Its loud buzzing and humming bounced from its four propellers as it hovered above their heads. Higher and higher the drone went, until it was just a blip in the sky, way above all those willow trees that surrounded their homes. Now Kisha was ready to show them what they had come for. They all gathered closely to see the screen. At first it was hard to see, then the picture cleared up, and they could all see it clearly.

## A LARGE DOSE OF PERSPECTIVE

Death and dying have a strange way of cultivating perspective in our lives. We all know this from the tumultuous COVID-19 pandemic in 2020. The fear, permanence, and uncertainty of death force us to broaden our perspective about life and what really matters. Perspective is also necessary for transformative movement building, and it is a key ingredient for healing-centered leadership. Stephen Bennett didn't know that death would compel him to live, transform his leadership, and play a key role in launching the AIDS activism movement during the 1980s.

Now Stephen lives in a beautiful comfortable home in Palm Springs, California, with his partner, Mehi, but his life wasn't always comfortable. He is in his sixties now, but with his white precision-groomed beard and stylish swag, it's hard to tell his age exactly. He is a gay white man, and he speaks with a certified confidence that only comes with assured privilege—he can't help it. He isn't unaware, though, and doesn't hide behind the fact that his whiteness comes with unlimited social capital. He just chooses to spend it in the right places.

Coming out as a gay man was both freeing and terrifying for Stephen. During the 1980s he was married with a daughter and was unhappy with where his life was headed. He was a workaholic and was using drugs to escape the grind of work life responsibilities. He was a child of the '60s, and sexual exploration and a little bisexuality were accepted. But his desires and attraction to men slowly became an issue because he was married and had a beautiful daughter and a promising career. He simply didn't have room in his life to be gay. He decided to visit John, a friend and therapist, in his North Hollywood apartment to get a grip on things. It wasn't long before Stephen began to see his life from a different perspective as he recounted to me during our interview.

> *It was like jumping into an abyss because we have this percep-*
> *tion of who we are and that's how we move through the world,*
> *and it's how the world responds to you. Then, all of sudden, I*
> *had perspective of who I was pulled out from under me entirely.*
> *I had to recreate who I was and build a new perspective about*
> *how I see the world. Most of my life, I had these negative stereo-*
> *types of gay men, and I just felt like I jumped off a cliff and I*
> *didn't know if there would be a bottom to it. That happened in*
> *the early '80s, and of course AIDS was just getting started. So*
> *it was not an exact time you wanted to be dating and sexually*
> *active. On top of all that, I had a daughter to raise.*

There is a lot of shame to work through that comes with being openly gay and, at the time, not a lot of places to heal from the turmoil of coming out. His brother was there for him and helped him with one of the most important lessons he has learned. His brother told him, "You can recreate yourself! You can create the person you really want to be, and few people ever get to do that. But you can!" That's the privilege you get from coming out: you get to recreate yourself, recreate your relationships, and show up as a new authentic person. For so long, we all practice and learn to be something that may not be our true authentic selves. We try to be more articulate, we pretend to care about people, we want to be seen as important, because we are searching for some authenticity that is already inside of us.

That's exactly what Stephen did, and by 1988 he had become the CEO for AIDS Project Los Angeles, perhaps one of the most public and controversial AIDS advocacy organizations in the country. On his first day, he walked into a 40,000-square-foot warehouse near Santa Monica Boulevard. There were offices in the front, but most of the building was used for the organization's food bank. His office was large but simple. He had a dark brown wooden desk, where he placed a large bowl of gold-coin condoms to promote safe sex and public health. That job changed his life and altered his perspective about how life really works.

For the next ten years, Stephen cultivated perspective from watching suffering and death from being close up to sick clients, as they sweated in his office from fevers, as they tried to find medical care, as they were rejected by family and friends. But he also had to raise money for his organization by speaking to wealthy entertainers at prestigious fundraisers. Being close and distant at the same time gave him both precious intimacy and a bird's-eye view of the AIDS movement in Los Angeles that made all the difference in his perspective about justice and how to achieve it. He recalled a typical morning on the job.

*There was a guy in West Hollywood who had been ill and near the end, and he had gone on a crystal meth binge for three days. At the end of the three days he took a gun and shot his brains out. No one had heard from him in a few days, so his mother finally went over and opened the door and found him with his brain spread out all over the apartment. So his mother called our agency and said, "I don't know what to do." The agency's case manager went over to support the family; she kept calling around to find a mortuary that would come get the body. Nobody wanted to pick up the body. Finally, our agency found a mortuary way out in Sylmar, and they said they would come pick him up if we would give him $500 in cash and have the body in a bag. So the mother and the case manager went to get the money, and the mortuary finally showed up and took the body away. The case manager returned to our office with another sick client waiting for her. That was a normal day.*

There is something about death that burns away all the bullshit, leaving clarity in its wake. Dealing with death close up and far away gave Stephen a perspective about life, justice, and movements that few people ever see. He used to think that his job as CEO for the largest AIDS organization in the country was to be a tactical and strategic leader. After all, his MBA was from UCLA and had covered all the nuts and bolts about leadership and organizational change. Despite his training, however, nothing had prepared him for the type of leadership that was needed to build a movement in America for compassion and support of people who were dying of AIDS.

Over the course of ten years, just about everyone he knew died from AIDS, and it was one of his most life-changing experiences. He commented, "Most of my days as CEO had nothing to do with me, it was about other things that I had not been trained for, and I'm not sure anyone can be trained to lead that way. I had to step up way beyond what I considered to be my capacity. I had to change from thinking and perspective about my role as a tactical leader. But I wasn't sure what that meant." Stephen didn't have the luxury of relearning, revisiting his management textbooks, nor of attending the latest Harvard Business School workshop about managing through crisis. No, people were dying, and he needed to learn to pivot in his perspective about what was needed for him, his organization, and the AIDS movement.

*I would get to the office in the morning and call everybody together, review the financials, do a management team meeting. Then I would go to a fundraising lunch and walk in and say to the head of one of the recording studios, "We really need your record label to support our event and we need $100,000 and I need at least three celebrities that you've signed on. We need this to address AIDS in this city." Then I would leave lunch, go back to the food bank, where there would be 150 people waiting in line, and we would do a memorial service for everybody who died that week. Half of my staff died the first year, and that's not talking about clients, that is just my staff! There was about four or five deaths a week, so we would hold a joint memorial service* *around four o'clock. Then at 5:30, I would be at a cocktail party raising money. Just about everybody I knew died. I was going to three or four funerals a week plus the memorial service.*

There is only so much compassion and empathy that a leader can have in situations like this. As Stephen says, empathy and compassion can only get you so far as a leader. If you're not careful, you can be overwhelmed and swallowed up by the enormous severity and surreal nature of what's happening. Stephen could only see the elephant's trunk and had mistaken it for a snake. He was peering through a hole in the fence and concluded that what he saw on the other side was the entire story. He needed a pivot in his perspective to be the type of leader that could be effective.

*During that time, I was feeling like I needed to step outside of my prescribed role as a CEO, and I needed to even step outside of Stephen Bennett. I needed to see what was happening as a healer and as someone who could fight for justice, raise funds, while at the same time bring deep compassion to those who were suffering. You know, every minute I needed to be a healer in every interaction. People would come screaming in my office, and I knew that they were dying, you know, they probably wouldn't live three more days. What people needed from me was a sense of purpose, dignity, and peace.*

But saying a shift in perspective is important is much easier than doing it. Stephen admits that most of the time he was in a fog, and being there for other people didn't give him the time for his own grieving. He commented,

*I didn't have time to do my own grieving, and I still suffer from it. There was no time for my own grieving. I remember one evening after work, a friend of mine, John, who was very ill. He was a very sweet guy, and his family had disowned him. He lost his home, he lost his job, and he was living in a small apartment in Santa Monica. He was a pianist and owned a beautiful piano, and he called me and asked me to come by. When I arrived I saw that his piano was gone. He told me he had to sell it that day to pay his rent and get some food. But by the time I got there, he was laying in bed, it was soaking wet, he was shivering. It was horrible the way he died. I took care of him and cleaned him up and stayed with him and held him for a while. And those were the moments that change you forever.*

As Stephen shared this story with me, he looked away, took a deep breath, and exhaled. He was choked up, but he couldn't hold back the emotional toll from all the years of loss he had known and not fully processed. He began to cry, and his precious humanity spilled out. He had not recovered from the years of pain, confusion, and death that had defined his leadership. He was still grieving. While the extreme stress from his past experience still weighs on him today, something about being simultaneously close up and far away from the AIDS movement made him appreciate the moment. Not enjoy it, nor hate it, but appreciate the fact that he was able to help so many people who were dying of AIDS. There were a lot of people who felt helpless, and all they could do is watch their loved ones die; at least as the leader of AIDS Project Los Angeles, he could help.

*So when I would go see people like John who were near the end, or spend time with people on staff or personal friends who were dying, those last few days, months, days, weeks, hours, you move from a transactional relationship to transformative relationship; it gives you a different perspective on life and work. Because you get to know somebody much better in those last three weeks than you knew them for the last ten years. You're sitting with them, they're laying in bed. You know they're dying. You know they're in discomfort. We're talking with them about maybe assisted suicide. Maybe we're talking about communicating with their moms. We're talking about how they feel about things. Like, "John, you had to sell your piano today, are you OK?" "No, I'm not OK." You in those moments gain a deep appreciation for people, for life, and move past the surface shit.*

# MORE THAN FUNERALS AND FUNDRAISING

Death had cultivated in Stephen a close-up, hole-in-the-fence view and a bird's-eye view of the AIDS movement. That's why the COVID-19 pandemic of 2020 wasn't the first time he witnessed how an unseen virus can transform a society. Except this time, the virus wasn't labeled gay-related immune deficiency (or GRID) like it was during the 1980s. During the early phases of the AIDS epidemic, President Ronald Reagan refused to say the word *AIDS* for the first three years. There was little to no federal response to the crisis, and nobody was coming to the rescue. As Stephen remarked, "We had to come to our own rescue."

Being simultaneously close up and far away from the AIDS movement allowed him to shed the fear that sometimes holds us back and to gain the courage to imagine another way. Stephen began to work closely with ACT UP, Queer Nation, and the other AIDS organizations that formed the big six, the six largest AIDS agencies in the world. Together the leadership of these six organizations would meet every six weeks to reimagine how to reshape the movement.

*We realized that we needed to change the perception of AIDS in America. So we decided that we had to work with the entertainment industry. So we worked with studios in Los Angeles, and then New York would follow because they had the theater business. But in Los Angeles we had the movie industry and the music industry, and so we leveraged that like crazy to make it very cool and edgy to be involved in AIDS. And it worked! All that death gave me a new perspective to see what was wrong with the movement, and a vision for what it needed. So I worked with folks and channeled it into a type of leadership that would rebrand AIDS in America.*

Stephen came to realize that his job as CEO was more than funerals and fundraising. There comes a point where death and dying rip away all of the surface stuff and push us into a new way of seeing old problems. "After a while I started to shed my fear of what people thought about me, losing my job, hurting my feelings, and not being accepted. I just didn't give a fuck, and that perspective is so damn freeing!" His perspective allowed him to see his work as rebranding the negative perceptions of gay and lesbian communities held by the public at large. By 2005 the movement that had begun as AIDS activism had transformed the rights for same-sex marriage. This transformation around how we viewed AIDS prompted a revolution in the support of same-gender loving. Ten years later, in 2015, the US Supreme Court made same-gender marriages legal in all fifty states.

Not all of us get the opportunity to change how people think about the issues we seek to change. Most of us work every day to improve some aspects of our society. But have you paused to simply ask, Am I looking at this issue through a hole in the fence? Do I have a bird's-eye view of the issue I seek to change? Perspective, in our journey toward justice, is critical in our ability to reimagine and not just react, and in our capacity to transform and not just respond. We have to learn to be close up, to see and smell the sweat, yet far enough above to really see why people are sweating. Both vantage points are important, and neither is right nor wrong, but rather together they are more complete.

\* \* \*

As they gathered around the screen, Malcolm, Javier, and Vien were amazed at what they saw. The camera on the drone high above allowed them to see a more complete view of Kisha's backyard creation. Now it was clear to all of them that what they saw from their fences wasn't entirely correct but not entirely wrong, just incomplete.

Vien saw the structure come into view first. "It's a tree house with a yellow door!" she exclaimed. Javier saw it as well and said, "Yes, a tree house with a deck—that's pretty cool, Kisha!" Finally, Malcolm saw why he had seen ropes and the bow of a boat. "I can see now—you've made the tree house in the shape of a boat. Wow, that is really cool."

"The tree house is for my children, who absolutely love boats," Kisha said. "I thought, why not create something where they can play and imagine? I've been working on the design for a long time. When the construction is finished, I would love to have your children all play on it as well."

## FOUR CONDITIONS FOR CULTIVATING PERSPECTIVE—BUILD YOUR TREE HOUSE

Perspective is about seeing close up and far away at the same time. Being close up gives us the nuance and a deeper understanding of how poverty, racism, and homophobia impact people, families, and communities. Yet we also need a bird's-eye view to understand the root and systemic causes underneath it all. Again, neither is right nor wrong, good nor bad, just incomplete. Seeing the entire elephant means that we take into consideration our own assumptions about the conclusions we make. Just like how Nedra concluded that the Lyft driver must be conservative and have racist views because he didn't respond to her questions didn't mean that she was wrong; her assumption could be true. Yet her assumptions weren't entirely correct either, because he was deaf. In the same way, we have to be relentless in examining our assumptions and work to build greater perspective in our work.

Systems-change researchers have done a good deal of research on ways that we can build our ability to have perspective in the work we do to change our society. Systems-change researchers have identified five conditions that allow leaders to cultivate perspective. The best way to imagine these conditions is to imagine an iceberg with four levels. At the tip of the iceberg are events, things that happen in systems. The next level down is patterns, which are trends that occur over time. Going deeper, the next level of the iceberg is structures, which are the relationships that create the patterns. Finally, at the deepest level of the iceberg are mental models, which are the assumptions, beliefs, and values we hold.

Most of us try to create lasting and durable social change by reacting to events, the "hole in the fence" in our work. We react to racial injustice and respond to attacks on immigrant communities.

Think about just about any social issue that you want to change, and it's likely based on some event. Take for instance Steven's initial response to men dying of AIDS in the 1980s; at first he was simply responding to events—funerals and fundraising. But it was his reflections about death that pushed him further down the iceberg. He began to identify trends and patterns that were the underlying causes of death. Moving even further down the iceberg, he recognized that ultimately the structure that supported these patterns was the refusal on the part of policy makers to even discuss the AIDS epidemic. Finally, he realized that he needed to work at changing the mental models that people held of the disease itself and their perceptions of gay and lesbian communities.

This can be a tool that helps us cultivate greater perspective in our work for justice. It improves our ability to get close up and elevates our ability to see above the issue we are trying to change. We can ask some simple questions: Am I responding to an event? What are the patterns and trends I see with this issue? What are the underlying structures and relationships that support these patterns? What assumptions do I hold about this issue? Let's use Nedra's response to the Lyft driver to see how this process could help her gain more perspective in that specific situation.

|  | HOLE-IN-THE-FENCE VIEW | BIRD'S-EYE VIEW |
|---|---|---|
| **EVENT** | Lyft driver doesn't respond to her "hello" | Lyft driver doesn't respond to her "hello" |
| **PATTERN** | White men don't acknowledge Black women | The driver did not hear her |
| **STRUCTURE** | White supremacy | His hearing is impaired |
| **MENTAL MODEL** | He is racist | He is deaf |

Now, it could also be true that the Lyft driver was both racist and deaf. The simple point here is that we gain perspective when we go deeper than responding to events and explore the patterns, structures, and mental models that we respond to. So how do we build the capacity to gain perspective in our work? This is not to suggest that we need to learn how to discount racism, disregard bigotry, and ignore oppression when we see it. What I'm suggesting is quite the opposite, because when we address these issues with perspective, we can see the entire problem, not just the event.

This is not just an exercise about how we interpret things. There is an important distinction between interpretation and perspective. Interpretation occurs when we assign meaning to something and accept it as the entire truth. This is what happened with Nedra and the Lyft driver. Perspective, however, is an awareness of our and other viewpoints, and it means that we bear witness to other potential interpretations without judgment. Perspective means that we become the observer, the watcher of our own and others' potential interpretations.

This pivot in our perspective means that we have to interrogate our mental models, question our assumptions, and ponder our meaning making about events we see in the world. Until we do this, we will continue to respond to events stemming from racism, homophobia, and sexism because we have failed to examine America's collective mental models about who belongs and who deserves. It's like we will continue to play whack-a-mole with injustice because we haven't dealt with the root causes of what creates injustice in the first place—the deeply held mental model of who is human, who belongs, who deserves.

Perspective means that we all interrogate these questions in every moment and that we become the observer of our own assumptions. One way to do this is to take the perspective of a third position. In the case of the Lyft driver, Nedra was first position, the driver was second position, but Nyah enjoyed third position because she observed both and had the perspective to respond in the most informed and insightful way.

These tools are not easy, and from time to time I fall into the trap of losing my perspective. But pivots are not easy, yet they are worthwhile. More importantly, when we begin to courageously practice pivots in our perspective together, we recreate a society where everyone belongs and a world basking in the joy of justice.

# 8

# *Possibility*

L ateefah could smell cigarette smoke and vodka from downstairs creeping up the stairway, past the bathroom, and into her bedroom. Her mother always told her and her little sister to go to bed just before the adults began a night of smoking and drinking. Even at ten years old, Lateefah knew that when people would knock on the back door of their Fillmore flat, they were there to buy drugs. Her mother was loving and caring, but she worked a lot, and when she came home from work, she wanted to relax with friends and enjoy a drink and a Kool cigarette. During the mid-1980s drugs began to dramatically transform the Fillmore district in San Francisco, and these same drugs altered Lateefah's life forever. "My mother loved us, but wasn't checking on us," Lateefah commented to me in an interview. So as a teen, she stayed out of the house as much as she could, choosing to stay with friends or spend the night with her boyfriend. She wanted to be anywhere but home.

When Lateefah was a high school senior, her family received an eviction notice. While this came as a shock to Lateefah, apparently her mother had not paid rent in years. The landlord allowed her family to continue living in their home because he cared for Lateefah.

But by her senior year, the landlord had had enough. Lateefah's senior year proved to be a challenging and complicated time, starting with the day of their eviction: the moving van that contained all of their belongings was stolen because her mother neglected to watch the truck. Lateefah attended one of San Francisco's best high schools and enjoyed being on the debate team, all the while living in the projects and watching her boyfriends sell drugs. It wasn't long after high school that she fell in love with a beautiful young man, he proposed to her, and she gleefully accepted. Then one night he tried to kill her. They didn't have a heated argument or a fight, not even a yelling match. But out of the blue, he snapped and calmly told Lateefah that he was going to kill her. Before she had a chance to process what he'd said, he hit her on the right side of her face so hard it split her lip wide open. Then he strangled her with his big hands and wouldn't let go; she couldn't breathe.

> *I saw that white light, you know that people say when they are about to die, well, I saw it! He started strangling me and I literally let go. Then I saw myself, literally saw myself, on the bottom of that floor with blood coming down my nose. He collapsed on my body and he started sobbing because he realized that he was killing me. But my first thought was, "Who's gonna find me, my body?" There was a certain grace and a clarity that I felt. I didn't panic, or even try to fight back, I was just pragmatically thinking about details about the aftermath.*

It all happened in slow motion. First she thought about who had the keys to the apartment, who could raise her three-year-old daughter after she was gone? Maybe one of her close friends would realize that Lateefah had not answered her phone in a few days and drop by her apartment, or maybe someone from work would find it strange that she just didn't show up and would come by after a couple of days. Just as she was working through all the details and logistics of her tragic departure, she came to. She was alive. She touched her face; it felt strange. So she crawled to the mirror. Her eyes were swollen shut, and she could barely see that her face looked like a basketball. She felt like she had died and come back to life for a second chance. Lateefah Simon's next thought was, "I'm gonna live, I'm actually gonna live . . . I'm about to get free."

It was the one and only time in their relationship that he had been physically abusive to Lateefah. Somewhere deep inside she knew something else was going on. Turns out, though, that her partner had an underlying condition that he had been keeping from her. He suffered from schizophrenia and hadn't had his medication. Surviving the trauma of this physical abuse incident opened up another possibility for Lateefah. She had been working and living with fear. It was invisible at first, but she knew fear was always present, always whispering in her ear, "You can't, you shouldn't, you won't." She was an activist, an advocate for young women of color, and was the youngest executive director of the Center for Young Women's Development in San Francisco. Turns out this was the same organization that had supported her during her tumultuous teenage years. Despite her outspoken advocacy, and her dedication to fight for the rights of young women in San Francisco, she hadn't felt free.

We may not all share Lateefah's tragic story, but we can all relate to the feeling of not being free—bound to the rules of our society, locked into the responsibilities of our work, and tethered to obligations to our families. We are all silent and obedient to our invisible fears. Lateefah's horrific abuse prompted her to pivot from merely surviving and seeing the world as a place to endure. She refused to just cope with all the problems that came with poverty, oppression, and suffering. She made a pivot to see the world as a place of possibility and began to imagine a potential future, one that she would create.

In 2003 Lateefah Simon won the MacArthur "Genius" award for her groundbreaking work with young women with histories of abuse, drug addiction, prostitution, criminal records, and living on the streets of San Francisco. She knew that these young women were smart and just needed opportunity, healing, and guidance. So she hired as mentors the same women they served, gave them steady income and job skills. She pioneered a number of strategies that engaged young women in advocacy and leadership development.

For the next ten years, she grew the organization from serving approximately 200 women to about 3,500 women per year and employed more than 250 women in the city. She also expanded her efforts beyond San Francisco and worked to change public policy at the regional and state levels. She spearheaded San Francisco's first anti-recidivism youth services division under District Attorney Kamala Harris. In 2016 Lateefah was elected to serve District 7 on the Bay Area Rapid Transit (BART) board of directors, and in 2020 she was voted president of the board. In 2016 she was also appointed to the California State University Board of Trustees. Today she is the chief executive officer of the Akonadi Foundation and is leading the organization's efforts to address racial inequality through organizing and building power among young people of color. She commented,

> *That's what freedom journeys are about. You go through things and you come out on the other side not frozen by fear, even when it shows up. Like Harriet Tubman, it's not just about getting slaves to run away toward freedom, but it was also about contemplating freedom itself. Like the physical reaction your body goes through knowing that there's nothing that you can do but surrender, or knowing what it feels like to be at the grocery store, not having enough money to get all that you want. It helps me make decisions every day and helps me give people grace. It makes me remember that I'm not the only one who'd been beat down and bloody. Our grandmothers and great-grandmothers struggled, and they had a deep vision for me way before I got here. They had a vision and an imagination of freedom before they even knew what it looked like.*

This is not a story about overcoming abuse and thriving, nor is it about succeeding against the odds. Naw, there are enough Horatio Alger stories out there, and this isn't another one. This story is about freedom and possibility and the role they play in our lives and work for justice. I'm not sure how many of us really contemplate freedom, because so much of our time is focused on solving intractable problems and fighting for justice. But our inability to contemplate freedom and lean into a possible future is one of the most significant barriers we face in creating justice. Somewhere along the way we have learned to talk about problems, measure the problem, and finally define the misery that comes along with the problem itself. Lateefah's story shows us that while violence, poverty, and oppression impact us, they should never define us. The struggles that people face are real, yet our histories do not determine who we are nor limit our agency. We can create the future we wish to see rather than simply eliminating the present conditions we need to change. For those of us working to improve our society, we have to take seriously our capacity to see beyond the challenges we face and the problems we need to solve. It is critically important that we dream and imagine as well as fight and resist. But first, before we abandon our daily efforts to solve intractable problems in our communities, we need to better understand the problem with problems.

## THE PROBLEM WITH PROBLEMS

It's really hard to dream when we are fighting for justice. The issues we care about are all urgent, life threatening, and entrenched. So how does our imagination and dreaming help address the problems people face on a daily basis? There are a lot of problems in the world to be solved, and it's likely that you are working to solve one of them. Maybe you are an educator trying to improve educational outcomes for your students, or you are an executive director of a nonprofit organization working on behalf of immigrant rights. You might be an entrepreneur who has created a company that provides internet access to remote places in the world. Most of you reading this are working to solve an important social problem in the world. The fact is that we all need to be in the business of solving social problems. There would be no human progress without our collective social problem solving. But we often see problems more clearly than we can imagine solutions to them. It's often easier for us to name, identify, discuss, and articulate problems than it is for us to imagine entirely new solutions. Trista Harris, author of *FutureGood: How to Use Futurism to Save the World*, calls this "problem loving," which is the tendency for leaders to assume that awareness of the problem is the same as solving it. Leaders often are trained to clearly articulate the problems they are facing in their sector. The myth of problem loving is that knowledge of the problem is all we need to solve it. We think we're fixing the problem by understanding how bad the problem is!

Take for instance my own training as a sociologist. My entire training generally focused on understanding the deep and often hidden social forces at work that maintain, reinforce, and reproduce social problems. My own particular expertise of problem loving is in education. I learned just about every possible way to explain why students of color from low-wealth neighborhoods performed poorly in school compared to their white counterparts. I have studied theories about why students of color perform worse in school, and I've even created my own theories and have tested them. For years I attended conferences to present my findings about educational problems without much consideration about ways to actually solve them.

I recall conducting a training with school principals about the racial differences in academic outcomes among their students. I had prepared my PowerPoint with slide after slide of evidence that proved there were dramatic differences in performance across the racial groups in their schools. I had them break out in small groups to discuss the tons of data that I had proudly presented. When they returned to the large group, one of the principals asked me a simple question. "Can you provide us with some solutions to these racial disparities in academic outcomes?" I had convinced myself that my job was simply to illustrate the problem they had in the district; I hadn't considered the possibility of providing solutions. So the question puzzled me, because my assumption was that once they understood how significant the racial disparities were in their schools, the principals and teachers would come up with solutions on their own. I was wrong.

# OPPRESSION IS THE ROOT
# OF PROBLEM LOVING

The problem with problem loving is that we become satisfied with discussing the problem and uncomfortable with imagining solutions. This is of course by design, and it's how oppression works! The conditions of oppression and the challenges of everyday life force us into daily survival mode and ongoing crisis management. Survival caused by oppressive conditions renders our imagination inert. We are all in an abusive relationship with oppression, and rather than leaving the relationship altogether, we choose to fight it. Oppression says to us, "All you can do is resist and fight me. But you will never leave me altogether," and this is precisely what we unconsciously do, unaware of our abusive relationship with oppression. Oppression has forced us to only solve problems, locking us into a way of thinking that keeps us in the same predicament. No fundamental change has ever come from problem fixing. We only reform and repair systems, institutions, and social relationships. There is no radical transformation.

During one of my graduate seminars years ago, I highlighted this point to my students. I wanted to push them away from problem loving and into possibility creating. Many of them were organizers or community activists who were working on important issues in the San Francisco Bay Area. Some were advocates for affordable housing, others were organizing homeless families, still others were helping to build stronger police accountability with mothers whose children had been killed by the police. As I explained to them the problem with problems, some of them pushed back, as I always encourage my students to do. They argued that if they didn't fight for people's rights and build power, there wouldn't be any significant change. Fighting and resisting oppression for them was the only tool to bring the changes that they wanted to see. So I asked them to write a short one-page paper describing the problem they were addressing and how they were attempting to address it. Here is a sample of what they said:

- ▶ Fighting for police accountability in San Francisco's police department

- ▶ Resisting racist housing policies that force Black families from the city

- ▶ Confronting homophobia in schools

- ▶ Demanding anti-racist classrooms

- ▶ Struggling for environmental justice

I explained that our language sometimes holds clues to our problem loving. I noticed a pattern in the terms they used to describe their work. Most of their terms directly responded to the condition they wanted to change. Terms like *fight, resist, struggle, confront, defend* are connected to oppression, and they predefine the outcome of work in ways that fail to affirm what the students wanted to create or imagine. Next I asked them to rewrite the one-page description of their work, but they could not use any of the following words in the left-hand column, only the terms in the right-hand column:

| | |
|---|---|
| Resist | Reimagine |
| Defend | Dream |
| Disrupt | Discover |
| Demand | Create |
| Fight | Design |
| Struggle | Play |
| Confront | Invent |
| Destroy | Visualize |
| Deconstruct | Build |

The assignment was designed to push them into their imagination and use the language that affirmed it. They told me it was one of the most difficult assignments they had ever had because they had to really imagine what they wanted to see rather than articulate what they wanted to eliminate. They weren't used to using their imagination to address injustice, oppression, and inequality. In fact, the historian Robin Kelley reminds us in his book *Freedom Dreams* that imagination may be one of "the most revolutionary ideas available to us, and yet . . . we have failed miserably to grapple with [its] political and analytical importance."[1] This is why we need to be very careful in the terms we use to describe our work. If we are not thoughtful about our words, our work is confined and prescribed and fails to use our human condition to dream and imagine beyond oppression.

I think it was Dr. Cornel West who said that there is no affirmation through negation. We can never achieve what we want simply by pointing out what we don't. This is why I'm cautious about the term *anti-racist*. We should be mindful and avoid defining the world we want by articulating what we don't want. The absence of violence doesn't constitute peace, nor does the absence of illness constitute health. Peace is something entirely different from anti-violence; health and well-being cannot be adequately described as anti-illness. Light is not anti-dark, nor is water anti-land. These are important things in and of themselves. That's why *anti-racist* is akin to saying, "I anti-hate you so much, would you marry me?" rather than, "I love you, let's get married." Love is not simply anti-hate, and no one would enter a relationship defined in this way! In the same way, the term *anti-racist* simply falls short of naming precisely and affirmatively what we really want. The term *anti-racist* does a good job of articulating an active and engaged stance against racism (as opposed to the passive term *non-racist*) but fails to articulate a vision of what comes after that. Being non-racist and anti-racist are two sides of the "not" coin, which never gets us to what we really need and want, which is belonging.

*Belonging* perhaps comes closest to what comes after anti-racism. john a. powell, director of the University of California's Othering & Belonging Institute and professor of law and African American studies and ethnic studies, calls belonging "the circle of human concern," which is the expressive and institutionalized act of inclusion and mattering. More importantly, the word *belonging* is a term of affirmation and a statement of a potential desired future. *Belonging* and *inclusion* more adequately describe the world we want to create than the one we want to destroy. Now, of course an important prerequisite for belonging is anti-racism. We need folks to engage in an ongoing active stance to eliminate the attitudes, institutional structures, and privilege that come with whiteness. But belonging requires yet another step after we tear down the thick walls of racism. We need to build new bright and brilliant bridges of mattering and belonging where finally we can enjoy the profound and wonderful space of beloved community.

The idea of possibility is not new to our work toward freedom and justice. Take for instance enslaved Africans whose dream and imagination of freedom drove the Underground Railroad. Their profound capacity to dream of freedom even in the context of being enslaved conjured something more than abolition of slavery. "Freedom was for them, as it is for us now, a total transformation of society involving . . . new social relationships, new ways of living and interacting, new attitudes toward work and leisure and community."[2] What world are you dreaming about? We know what we are fighting against, but what are we creating, imagining, and fighting for?

## CREATING POSSIBILITIES

Possibility thinking and innovation are rooted in ancestral knowledge and Indigenous wisdom—they weren't created in the technology companies of Silicon Valley. I could dedicate an entire chapter to Indigenous people's innovative uses of plants to cure diseases, or skills with metallurgy far earlier than European exposure to the technology. It would take another chapter to illustrate African innovations ranging from the first twelve-month calendar with 365 days to the invention of mathematical notations used to construct the pyramids in Egypt. Innovation and possibility thinking can also emerge out of necessity: having to cure sickness without medical care or provide access to healthy food in a food desert. Echoing Green is one organization that recognizes that innovation often comes from those

closest to the problem. The group is dedicated to providing fellow-
ships and support to promising social innovators around the world
with leadership development and learning opportunities each year
for all their fellows.

So, our job is to lean into the practice of possibilities and strive
for the future we want to create. I know it's really hard given the
urgency, scarcity of resources, and limited time. But if we are in the
business of making deep change, we also have to transform what we
believe is possible. It's really the only way. We have to recognize how
oppression limits our vision and predetermines our actions and go at
it in a different way.

Not long ago, I was conducting a training with a group of organizations in a medium-size city in the Midwest. The leaders within
these organizations hadn't worked well together in years, and in fact
there was a great deal of distrust among them. The executive directors didn't trust the largest funder in the city, and the funder had
lost trust in some of the leaders. Many of the nonprofit organizations
battled over the scant resources the foundation provided, leaving
them underfunded and distrustful of one another. So when the foundation and one of the community organizations asked me to help
facilitate a healing process to restore trust and create a collaborative
process for the group of organizations, I jumped at the opportunity.

I usually take on projects like this too quickly. I don't ask the
right questions, I don't think about the real time commitment, and
I don't ask myself, "Is this something I should do?" When I began
working with the leaders in this city, the situation was worse than
I thought. My initial email to the group introducing myself was met
with a heavy dose of skepticism because I was an outsider, and there
was concern about why I was there in their community in the first
place. They were correct to be skeptical of me, an outsider who knew
very little about their community. I recall a video conference with
three executive directors who grilled me about who had asked me
to come to their city. The leaders pushed for a reason why I was
asked to work with these groups. Did I say the distrust was thick? It
was clear from my initial video conference that there was significant

skepticism, doubt, and unwillingness to engage in a conversation about creating a possible future. After a few months of my getting to know a few residents and building relationships with a few of the executive directors, we pulled together a community meeting with just about all the nonprofit leaders in the city. Even the police chief participated and spent time listening to our process.

During our first community meeting, I listened to residents raise concerns about the police, and many nonprofit leaders talked about the lack of funding they were receiving to support their work in the neighborhood. After the meeting, people pulled me to the side for a series of one-on-one conversations about why I shouldn't trust a particular person in the community, or why it was going to be impossible to do anything collaboratively. "Nothing you do will work here, Dr. Ginwright," they said, "people just can't see another way to work." Some said to me, "This community has a lot of trauma, and the trauma created a lot of hurt and distrust among some of the leaders here." The process that I had initially planned was supposed to take six months, but it actually took about two years.

During a subsequent meeting, just about everyone in the group talked about all the barriers to working together. They listed all the reasons why working together couldn't work and highlighted past failed attempts to restore community trust and collaboration. The group was entirely focused on problem loving and offered clear and compelling reasons why the collaborative effort would fail. Here are a few reasons I heard:

- ▶ "I don't trust organizations that receive all the funding but don't do any of the work in the community."

- ▶ "The foundation only funds the organizations they like; no one else can get funding to do the work."

- ▶ "There are always collaborations like this that come and go; this is just another one."

- ▶ "We already have a collaboration in the neighborhood; why do we need another one?"

- ► "We don't have the political power to do anything in this city because we can't get along."

- ► "Nothing will change until we establish more businesses; all of the businesses that used to be in the neighborhood are gone."

- ► "The powers that be will never allow efforts like this to succeed; they need us to continue to beg."

The truth is that the leaders of these organizations were struggling with small budgets, stressed from a litany of community problems, and frustrated by the inability to have a collective impact in the neighborhood. The condition of oppression had limited their ability to see anything outside of the daily survival to which they had become accustomed. There was no evidence, in their experience, that they could work together collaboratively on a common vision.

While the significance of the problem was important, the group also needed to pivot from problem loving to possibility creating. It was really hard at first because the harm was so deep that problem loving had become the only way they knew how to work together. I explained to the group how oppression harms us and makes us believe that we don't have the right to create, dream, and imagine. What we do instead is fight, resist, and confront, and while this is important, it's an incomplete toolkit for justice. We used a few practices to help the group lean into possibility thinking, and we introduced tools to help the group understand when they slipped into problem loving and how to get back to possibility thinking. Here are a few tools that we used.

## Word Play

We created one-hour blocks during our planning where we agreed to avoid phrases like "we can't, we don't, we shouldn't" and replace them with "we can, we do, we should." A pivot to possibility begins with an awareness of the language we use to describe our work. This activity also became a fun way for people to recognize and correct the words they used in our deliberations together. In fact there is a good deal of research about how language frames our reality, shapes our thinking, and influences our behavior.

## Future Forward

Events in the past have a way of limiting what we see in the future. It's a natural human tendency to learn from things in the past that were painful. If we aren't aware of how the past shapes our present thinking, however, we limit the possible future we wish to create. During our time, we played with the future! We asked people to use the prompt "what if" and complete the sentence with a bold and wild idea! The purpose was to rupture how past events shape future thinking and to open new possibilities. People said things like, "What if we created a multi-million-dollar fund for our organizations," "What if we acquired land and property for our work to serve our community," "What if we all went to Hawaii or some exotic warm island to do some planning together."

## Possibility Planning

*Design thinking* is a process that allows groups to see past the problem they are trying to solve and design a solution from people's actual lived experience. The process is really based in anthropology's research technique called participant observation, where we learn what people actually do rather than what they say they do in different settings. We used *possibility planning*, a modified design thinking process, where we asked members to bring their lived experience into the group and design solutions based on people's stories. When people shared the difficulty with obtaining funding or training staff, I asked them to use the term "how might we . . ." as a prompt to drive their thinking into solutions. The group developed statements such as

> ► *"How might we . . .* create a pool of funding that provides basic operating support every year to all of our organizations?"

▶ *"How might we . . .* build a cohort of leaders that understand how to run and operate businesses and community organizations?"

▶ *"How might we . . .* form a coalition where we are accountable to each other and not just the funding source?"

Notice the first word after "How might we" from each statement. "Create," "build," and "form" are all terms that lean into a future possibility. We used this process and other tools that moved the group in a few amazing ways. First, people began to self-correct themselves when they slipped into problem loving. They would say to each other when someone used problem loving language, "Is that possibility thinking or problem loving?" The question would gently redirect the conversation in a way that was focused on bold solutions.

Second, my team and I worked with the funder to provide support for a planning retreat in Hawaii. The purpose was to spend time healing relationships and chart a course of collaborative work in the city. Unfortunately, COVID-19 forced us to cancel the trip. The point is, however, all the members of the group were seeing a possibility of working together in new ways. Despite the fact that the retreat was canceled due to worldwide travel restrictions, we still gathered by Zoom once per month to heal from past injuries and dream about potential futures for the community. I didn't believe that healing could happen over Zoom video conferences. But we created the safety for people to share their personal challenges in their lives. Some of the members had become sick from the virus and were struggling to survive, and the group held them with love and light. Others in the group shared that their family members had lost jobs. The leaders in the group were creating a new future by healing from their past wounds.

Third, after nearly two years, the group began to imagine the possibility of advocating for and creating a city tax that would establish a designated pool of funding for their collective work. Together the group shared a vision of a way to work that could redefine their collective efforts. In a meeting with the funder, the community leaders

all shared what they had learned from their journey together. One of
the leaders passionately commented during the meeting:

> *There were so many times through this journey that I nearly
> cried. I didn't think it was possible, and now I know that achiev-
> ing our long-term vision lies with us! We can be angry with each
> other and continue to battle each other, but now I see folks here
> differently, and now I see that our healing process transformed
> how I see what's possible. I have to be honest with you, I didn't
> believe this healing was possible. I came to the first meeting
> because I wanted to get some money for my organization, not
> because I believed what Dr. Ginwright was saying to us. I was
> at our first meeting for some good food and to listen to this nice
> speaker from out of town, not because I believed change was pos-
> sible. I had long since given up on that idea, and I had given up
> on the community that I live in. Driving here today, I still see the
> dilapidated houses, the poverty on every corner, but my mind is
> different! For the first time in a long time, I believe in what we
> can do together in this community.*

The leaders gained a vision beyond simply improving their community; they transformed how they show up for each other and cultivated a sense of freedom to work together differently. One of the
members was an African American police officer in the community.
He discussed how challenging it was to be seen by the Black community as an "outsider" and his experience of racism within the police
department itself. He explained that he was wary and skeptical at
first because his training as an officer required that he not put on
rose-colored glasses but see problems for what they are. He shared
that being a part of the group was healing for him because he didn't
have space to dream or reimagine how the police could do better in
the community. He commented:

> *I needed this, because this process has absolutely changed me
> and has allowed me to see things differently! It works, and now
> that I have a community of people I can trust, and be real honest*

*with, and not worry that they won't love me because of my pro-
fession. I know they will hear me and hold me.*

Just like Lateefah, each of the members in the group said to
themselves "I'm about to get free" and could see a possible future.
I'll never forget what one member eloquently explained during one
of our meetings:

*When I began this journey, I was only walking by faith, not by
sight, because I just couldn't see where we were going. Now it's
like the fog is clearing, and I can see through the foggy mist in
the distance a mountain. That's where we are headed, but even
though I don't know how the hell we are going to climb that
mountain, I know that I won't be climbing it alone.*

# 9

# *Outlook*

*African American people have nursed nations of strangers, somehow saying, However you are, however backward you are in your humanness, I have the responsibility of treating you like a human being . . . the onerous task is to remember that the bigot, the brute, and the batterer are also children of god.*

MAYA ANGELOU, in *Restoring Hope* by Cornel West

I delayed writing this chapter not because I was struggling with what to say about the possibility of transforming our outlook about the world. Nor was my delay because of writer's block. I delayed writing this chapter because I was afraid of interviewing someone who is an amazing husband, a passionate football coach, a loving father, and a white nationalist. I had known "Big" John Brandon in high school, and we played football together during our teenage years. Football is his life. He was an offensive lineman at the University of Arizona and played semipro for a few years. Now at age fifty-three, he coaches football at a local high school in Southern California.

Turns out that John had read an op-ed piece I had published and posted on Facebook. He sent me a private message about how social media is blocking conservative speech. Then he would send me video clips, articles, and homemade news reports that promoted conspiracy theories like COVID-19 was caused by 5G. Then he sent me a private message that deeply disturbed me, and to be honest it scared me. He sent, in a text message, "The left acts in evil and selfish ways . . . when extreme things happen over and over, they become fact." He sent a picture of what appeared to be a white family who had been murdered in their car. The picture was so disturbing that I didn't read the article, and I blocked him from my account.

What bothered me most was his use of the term *evil* because once something or someone is considered evil, that justifies, condones, and even promotes its elimination. *Evil* is a term reserved for Satan, devil worship, and Hitler, not someone who holds progressive political views. That night, I stayed up thinking about what had compelled him to use the word *evil* in his message to me. I wondered what experiences had shaped his views. Did he truly believe that "the left acts in evil and selfish ways?" Has our country become so deeply divided that we see each other as evil, the ultimate form of dehumanization? You know when something happens and you just can't shake it from your mind? The event just keeps nagging around, and you mull over in your mind what you should have, could have done differently? Well, that's precisely how I felt when I discussed the event with my wife and a few close friends. I somewhat regret that I shared my dilemma with them because almost unanimously they said that I should reach out to "Big" John and interview him for this book!

At first I dismissed their suggestion as a sort of dare. But when they said to me that if I truly believe in healing and restoring our humanity as a nation, I have to practice what I preach so to speak. I've said before, "I have to see you as human, even if you refuse to believe that I am." My friends pushed me to live up to that statement and to reach out to those folks that I don't agree with. That's a lot easier said than done, but I knew deep inside that their challenge to me was correct because it's easy to share ideas of healing, belonging, and relationships with those that share your worldview. But what about those that you don't agree with? How do we cultivate an outlook that allows us to listen to each other without judgment and try to see our mutual humanity across difference? How do you listen to someone that holds beliefs about people of color that are dehumanizing, or political views that harm people, or attitudes that exclude? That shit is hard, real hard, which is precisely why I decided to reach out to interview him.

This chapter is about how our pivot from problem to possibility must include our outlook, the attitudes and values about a potential future. Our perspective (chapter 7) and ability to see possibilities (chapter 8) are supported and fueled by our outlook and deeply held vision and sense of our collective future. Leadership in times like these requires that we examine the entrenched ideas about the future and explore ways to mend the wounds of the present. A pivot to possibility is more than having rose-colored glasses on and a positive view of the future. Outlook involves exploring our fears, concerns, and pain without getting stuck in the existential mud. Our outlook is born in how we see the world and is made stronger in our efforts to contribute to something worthwhile.

I wanted to write this chapter to push my own assumptions about the world and test my own capacity to see something different. The challenge my wife and friends presented frightened me because I wasn't sure that my own outlook would be enough to listen to and interview someone who doesn't share my outlook of the world and is in opposition to my own values and commitment to justice. I told myself that such an interview wasn't a good use of my time because John wasn't going to advance any ideas in my book. For a few months I told myself that the idea to interview him was just plain unwise. What if he says something racist, completely uninformed, or inflammatory? I procrastinated for months until one day I decided to unblock John and invite him to be interviewed. I really wanted to know about his life, his views, and if I could learn something about myself in the process. So I sent John this message, "Hey

John - I'd really like to interview you for a new book I'm writing. It's not about politics, it's more about how we all can create a better society together. Are you open to a conversation and interview?" He replied immediately, "Hell yeah!"

## THIRD POSITION

I think that one of the skills I've developed over my career is the capacity to observe, listen, and watch people without judgment. I suspect it came from years of teaching students in my African American studies courses about race and racial inequality. Inevitably, I would encounter white students who would challenge me or question the material we would discuss in class. Because I encourage students to form their own opinions and conclusions, I always create space in my classes for open dialogue and discourse. This means that when students, usually white students, challenge ideas like "structural racism," "meritocracy," and "implicit bias," I always open up space for them to be heard. Even when students make racist comments, I've learned not to get triggered, and I calmly call attention to how their comments may insult, harm, or hurt others. I remember early in my career during one class, a white young man refused to call me Dr. Ginwright, or Dr. G as many students do. Rather, he referred to me as "Dogg," like "What's up, my Dogg?" or "Dogg, I don't understand the assignment." The Black students in my class immediately would openly scold him for disrespecting a Black professor. So one day in my office, I explained to him that calling me Dogg was inappropriate and perceived to be disrespectful by folks in class. He began calling me Dr. G like everyone else, but I never became emotionally attached to the incident. I just sort of observed it from a distance and watched it play out.

My students have said to me, "How can you not get angry at some of the racist comments that students say in class?" and "How do you put up with ignorant comments from students who have no clue about race?" I believe that learning happens best when we are curious about how other people think and students feel safe enough to disagree with each other. It takes time to build safety and trust in a classroom or workshop about race, but one of the most valuable lessons I've learned is to observe my emotional response to student comments in class. It's not that I don't get triggered, angry, or upset at some comments, because I do, particularly comments harmful and insulting to others. When that happens, learning stops. So I've learned to take a third position in classes and workshops where people disagree.

There are always three positions when people share ideas in classrooms, workshops, or trainings. *First position* is a particular outlook on any given topic that you believe is correct, accurate, valid, and true. We all speak from first position when we are in an argument with someone, or a disagreement or debate. First position allows us to have clarity about our point of view and helps shape our outlook. Think of first position as a held assumption that influences your outlook. For example, first position about gun control in the United States might be that all Americans have the right to bear arms as guaranteed in the Second Amendment in the Constitution. *Second position* is in opposition or counter to the first position. Second position is also based in a particular outlook that we believe to be true, correct, and valid. Second position may be that we all have the right to bear certain types of arms but not semiautomatic military-grade weapons. Second position pushes back against the first position with clarity, validity, and conviction. In a classroom, workshop, or training, conversations and debates generally volley back and forth between first and second positions, where both sides get stuck, where one side wins and the other loses. First position and second position are often competing to be correct, true, and valid—this is particularly the case when people speak from personal experience. These two positions are like dancing in cement, ultimately calcifying both views, permanently locked into a single outlook on an issue.

There is also, however, the *third position*, where someone simply observes both first and second positions. The goal of third position is to watch from some distance the volley between first and second positions from a place of curiosity, without judgment. Taking third position doesn't mean that you don't have an opinion; it just means that you are aware of your opinion and emotional response to what is occurring. It's like an American watching a game of rugby or cricket. If you aren't familiar with these sporting events, you might watch the game out of curiosity in order to learn, understand, and identify the rules. You are more curious about what's happening than you are about who's winning.

When I decided to talk to John, the white nationalist I knew from high school, I didn't want to be triggered, angry, or upset. I needed to pivot in my outlook, from opposition to curiosity, and that shit is really hard. So I took third position, and I did my best to listen to him, and to my own thoughts. I wanted to watch the game without judgment to see what I might learn about outlook.

## '66 MUSTANG

John had just restored his yellow 1966 Mustang and was on top of the world. He had his dream job as a head coach, and he and his wife had just delivered their first child. The Santa Ana winds had settled into Southern California, and as usual the warm dry air signaled that summer was over and the fall semester was back in session at Corona High School. As John drove past Vons grocery on Magnolia Avenue and West Ontario Boulevard, he didn't pay much attention to the color of the leaves on the trees, nor the fact that the days were getting shorter. He had planned to get to school early so that he could prepare the lesson for the typing class he was teaching. It was strange that Leslie, his wife, would call him on the way to work, so he decided to answer her call while he was driving. She was crying. Madison, their newborn, was sick. Leslie had found blood in Madison's diaper and their precious child was limp and not responding.

John pulled over and came to a screeching stop and made plans to meet Leslie and Madison at the hospital. Turns out that the child was born with a severe heart defect—the arteries to her heart were switched. Dextro-transposition is a rare heart defect where the two main arteries that bring blood in and out of the heart are reversed in their locations; blood comes in where it should be going out and vice versa. Few infants survive surgery after the first year. To make matters worse, Madison had developed an infection that was even more threatening than the heart condition. Before they could repair the child's heart, they needed to treat the severe infection that had taken over her digestive track. This was all before the doctors could perform open-heart surgery on an already fragile infant.

> *So there were days when I would go to work, then go to the hospital, finally I'd go home just to sleep and do it all over again the next day. It was a really tough few months for us, and it was definitely one of the lowest and most challenging times of my life. When you're going through something like that, you really don't understand the gravity of it. Unless it does happen to you. You know.*

He is correct; the experience of losing a child is unimaginable to most people. But for John and Leslie, this possibility wasn't fiction or theory. It was happening in real time, and there wasn't much the doctors could do to save her. A few weeks later, Leslie called John while he was still at work to prepare him for the worst. Leslie was at the hospital night and day, and the doctors had grown concerned that Madison's heart rate at 250 was a sign that she might not make it. John immediately left his class for the hospital and remembers walking into the hospital room and seeing his little child with a colostomy bag. He recalls watching his own life, his hopes and dreams, bounce up and down in green bleeps on the heart rate monitor. After several operations, and a long road of medications, Madison survived, with a few complications. Today she is a healthy young woman.

There are things that happen to us that change us forever and chart the direction for our outlook on life. For John and Leslie, as for any of us, the possibility of losing a child fundamentally changed them. They are both Christian, and both go to church, but during that ordeal, there was a deep sense of abandonment from God. Leslie had grown a bit mad at God and was asking questions like, "Why did this happen? I don't deserve this! We developed a certain amount of detachment." After the ordeal, John focused on football and was reminded of all the lessons he learned about life when he was playing. Probably the most important lesson he shared with me was that anything can be achieved through hard work and dedication. He shared story after story about his own hurdles in life on and off the field that he overcame through hard work.

> *The most important life lesson that I've learned over the years is that you can lose it at any time. Almost losing Madison taught me that. You learn to appreciate what you have, appreciate your friends and your loved ones and people you trust. Also on the field, I coach players about the importance of me putting others first, you know, work hard now means delayed gratification. When you play football, you get ten guaranteed games a year, and you work so hard all year for these ten games, so delayed gratification is tough, and some people just can't do it.*

When he played football in college, this lesson was reinforced by his own coaches, and more than anything, he sees success as the result of hard work and effort. He shared with me a story about what it took for him to get in shape for football and all the sacrifice required for him to perform on the field. He came to a point where he made a decision that he would never be out of shape, and that was it. He worked over the next year to lose weight and build muscle and was ready for the following season.

> *I was strong by the next season. This is what I have to do to be successful, and I learned that no matter how hard it gets, no matter what the situation is or what the obstacle is in front of you, if you want something bad enough, and you need it as if your life depended on it for survival, you're gonna find a way. The lessons I learned in those years are important to me. If I just put my mind to it and if I just sacrifice and work hard and work through the pain and do it. It's got to be done. Even if it's uncomfortable as hell!*

It's a lot easier to think about third position than it is to actually practice it. I wanted to explain to John the realities of structural racism, and how Black families worked hard, toiled in their soil only to have their land stolen. I wanted to tell him to read "A Case for Reparations" by Ta-Nehisi Coates in *The Atlantic*, or "The 1619 Project" in the *New York Times Magazine*. I wanted him to read about all the years of hard work Black farmers spent on their land only to have it stolen from them by white politicians through illegal means. I almost blurted out how whites were given favorable home loans that created generational wealth, whereas hard-working Black families were denied these same loans. I wanted to explain to him that all of this created generational caste-like Black urban poverty, not the lack of hard work!

Taking the third position, however, isn't interested in being correct, factual, and true, just curious and observant. So I watched my thoughts and listened to him share with me his story about the challenges with America. I braced myself and prepared for what I knew was going to be really difficult to listen to, hard to swallow, and challenging to hear. I had already given myself a pep talk and told myself, "Self, this is not a political debate, nor an opportunity to win over someone to your views. This isn't even a time for you to defend or rebuke anything that he shares. Just listen, Self." I did listen, and it was hard.

> *My main view of life, not just political views, is that I don't judge people, I only judge behavior. Behavior is what defines a person. It doesn't matter if they are white, Black, brown, whatever. I recognize that when you're the minority, you feel like you're being cheated. I understand that feeling because I was the one who was getting cheated when I was a kid. I was an outcast kind of, you know what I mean? Like I've been oppressed, so I understand and I'm sympathetic to it. But it's just not fair for people to be treated differently based on their race. I mean, I don't even like to bring color into it, but the left is always crying about racism, and it's not about race, it's about giving people shit that*

*they didn't earn. They don't deserve all this stuff if they don't*
*want to work for it! I get so pissed hearing Black people act like*
*a victim, and I'm like do something about it, don't just whine*
*about it and look for handouts.*

There it is! The moment I had been avoiding, fearing, and grappling with. He had expressed his view of Black people with honesty, clarity, and without apology. In his view, Black and brown folks were whining for handouts, lazy, and undeserving. As he explained his views he became visibly animated and almost agitated as if he was speaking from a place of disgust. He explained to me that he was mad at some of his Black friends because they are being manipulated by Democratic politicians. "The Democrats have been using Black people for their votes and have never delivered for Blacks, not even when Obama was president." He told me, "I fear if Biden becomes our next president." I remained curious and asked why he feared a Biden administration. He explained concerns about socialism and handouts to Mexican immigrants; he feared that the First and Second Amendments would infringe on his right to free speech and the right to bear arms.

There's only so much third position a brotha can take at a time, and for me, I was out of third position tokens and couldn't take it anymore. I abandoned the interview and cast third position away because, well . . . I wanted to tell him a few fears I had of my own!

## FEAR MIGHT SAVE US ALL!

I explained that my fears come from a different place, not about what freedoms I might lose (we never really had them). I explained that I have a fear that what we consider to be a democracy—healthy divisions and debate and engagement about what constitutes a citizen and a human being—is being shattered. I paused and explained that "my fear is that you think your fear is real." That's a fear that we've never had before, the fear of a new administration! When we share real fear and terror about an incoming government, that is a sign that our divisions are eroding the fabric of democracy.

I shared that my fear is that we are entering a space that is going to be hard to come back from unless we have more conversations like this. I explained my real fear is that our unchecked fear is going to destroy us all! I fear that the policies that we create will reinforce the wealth in this society and cement the rest of us into poverty. I fear that my tax dollars will go to corporations, who will have a greater voice than I do as a citizen.

John listened to me and was thoughtful in his response. He was quiet at first, and he rubbed his full graying beard as he pondered how to respond. He continued to share his fears about the divisions in our society. His outlook of American society was grim, unless conservative values became more central in our governing. He continued:

> So first of all, our freedom is starting to disappear, and our ability to make our own decisions is dwindling right now. Our country was built on the fucking Constitution and Bill of Rights, and those principles are not being practiced. We're getting further away from the founding principles, and people are thinking that they have a better way to do it. It's been working for 200 years, why do we need to fucking get rid of this thing? It's because this country is too hard for you? If you're poor, get out there and do something about it. Groups of people in this country want to just be victims and cry all the time about how things are just not fair enough. Now that's my fear, that we become a society that just rewards failure, that's just the liberal agenda.

Like I said, third position is really hard because there are millions of ways to respond to John's comments. But my goal wasn't to convince, debate, nor challenge but simply to listen, learn, and understand—did I say third position is difficult? The most difficult part of the interview came when he described his views about political leaders. During our discussion, he became visibly frustrated and commented that "Nancy Pelosi, goddamn, she is so damn evil." There is that term again. The one that kept me up at night, the term that deeply concerned me. He continued to describe the ways that she is leading with hatred when I jumped back into first position.

I abruptly stopped him and said that "when you use the term evil, John, that scares me because this is the term that Hitler used. Whenever you consider someone or something as evil, it justifies, condones, and encourages folks to remove evil from the earth, eliminate what and who is evil."

Without blinking, he replied, "Exactly, that she is evil in that way."

I was a little taken aback. He had confirmed that he didn't see Nancy Pelosi as fully human because of her evil deeds. That outlook really concerns me, not because people deeply disagree on the vision and direction of the country, but because we fail to see each other as human. I really didn't know what to say to John after that. So I listened to him for a while, and to be honest, I tuned out for a second, reflecting on his comments about Pelosi being evil. I suspect that it wasn't just Pelosi that he saw that way. I'm sure that he holds a list of other progressives that he would categorize that way.

I asked John to consider something. I asked him to imagine that Nancy Pelosi shared with him and Leslie a personal story of her own granddaughter. Imagine Pelosi got on national television, or maybe you listened to her on a podcast or something. Imagine that she shared, with emotion and passion, that she nearly lost her granddaughter to dextro-transposition, the same rare heart defect that his own daughter survived. Imagine that Nancy Pelosi explained in detail how she and her family felt helpless the same way he and Leslie felt, and that she was a little angry at God for letting it happen. Imagine she spoke from her heart about watching her hopes and dreams bounce up and down in green bleeps on the heart rate monitor. I asked him that if she shared such a story, how would he feel about her? John paused and sighed and rubbed the thick beard on his chin. He was relaxed now, and almost lost in his own thoughts. "I wouldn't wish that upon her, you know. If she shared that, it would impact me, because denying how she felt would be denying my own experience. It would shift me, man, if I heard her share that story, it would help me see her in a different light . . . I see where you are coming from."

I'm sure that John will never agree with progressive politics nor support progressive candidates. We don't share the same outlook. I do think it is possible, however, to explore ways to recast a different outlook, one based in a common sense of humanity. I think that our outlook—our attitudes, values, and vision about the future—has been like dancing in concrete, where our political and social divisions have gotten us stuck. A pivot to possibility means that we have to cultivate another outlook where we can see each other, even if we don't agree. I think the most important lesson I learned here is that we have a long road to healing our divisions. The greatest challenge before us is not simply a political, economic, or social transformation. Rather, the greatest challenge we face is failure to try another way. I know that taking third position is not a panacea to heal the wounds from the legacy of America's racial trauma, nor will it resolve continued harm caused by economic inequality. If we look deep within for a moment and ask how we can change our outlook, we will at least be on the right track. The pivot to possibility has to start within first. We have to all want something better for ourselves, our communities, and the world. I've heard someone say that if we want something we've never seen, we have to do something we've never tried, or something like that. I hope that we grapple with our own outlook on our society, that we'll try to strive to see the humanity in those folks who we vehemently disagree with. A pivot to possibility ain't easy, but who said that justice and peace would come easy, nicely wrapped in a bow?

# Pivot 4

## From Hustle to Flow

# 10

# *Flow*

*Clumsiness is grace in the making.*

JENNIFER JOHNS

had finally landed a meeting with a potential large funder of my work in early 1998, and I knew that the 9:00 A.M. Monday morning meeting I had arranged with the foundation was going to lead my organization to the funding we needed. On Monday morning I got up extra early to make sure I had enough time to get our one-year-old son, Takai, ready for daycare, get dressed, grab some coffee, and make it to the meeting with time to spare. But things really never work out as planned. I had dressed Takai and fed him his favorite breakfast. It didn't take long for him to spill his Cheerios all over himself, and now I needed to change him and get him something easier to eat. I thought to myself, *No sweat, it's just 7:30, and I still have time to drop him off at daycare, grab coffee, and get to my meeting by 9:00.* At 7:45 A.M. I grabbed my bag and my son, and we headed out the door. It was August, and the day hadn't warmed up, but I could tell it wouldn't be long before it was 85–90 degrees.

I placed Takai in the car seat and secured him with two straps (one for each shoulder) that lock into place by a large buckle that rests on his chest. As we pulled out of the driveway, I could see from the rearview mirror that he had somehow twisted himself out of the car seat and was trying to crawl freely in the back seat. It's 7:50 A.M., still plenty of time to get to my 9:00 A.M. meeting, so I pulled over to tighten the straps.

Finally, as I entered the onramp to the freeway, I could see that there was a lot of traffic, and I couldn't turn around to find a faster route, so I entered into the worst traffic jam I had seen in years! It was at a standstill, and at this rate, I wouldn't be able to drop Takai off at our daycare provider until 8:30. We sat and sat and sat in traffic, and it would be another thirty minutes to get to the meeting from the daycare facility. I thought to myself, "If I take him to daycare, then I risk being late to the meeting." So I came up with a brilliant idea! I would take him to the 9:00 A.M. meeting, have someone watch him during the meeting, and take him to daycare afterward! Now I'd be able to get downtown, find a place to park, and have plenty of time to make the 9:00 A.M. meeting.

Here's what happens next . . .

8:30    Arrive downtown Oakland

8:35    Drive around looking for parking

8:45    Find a parking spot!

8:50    Park car

It's almost 9:00, and now I'm basically late because I still have three blocks to walk to the office. So I kick into gear! Park car, find pay machine, pay for parking, grab son from back seat, walk fast to meeting . . . review key points of 9:00 A.M. meeting . . . I got this! As I swerved into the parking space, I swiftly unbuckled my seatbelt, grabbed a handful of quarters, quickly slid from the front seat—all in one well-rehearsed set of moves. I jammed a handful of quarters into the parking pay machine and swiftly walked back to my car to swoop up Takai. As I was in mid-stride, something struck me as wrong, like I forgot something important. So I went over a checklist in my head while still walking back to my car. Wallet—check, watch—check,

book bag—check, keys . . . keys—wait, where the hell are my . . . ?
I reached for the back door—locked. I grabbed the driver's door—
locked. That's when I realized that the entire car was locked with my
keys and one-year-old son securely trapped inside.

* * *

I'm sure we all have had moments like this when the pressure of
time collided with the demands of life, leaving you utterly helpless.
To some extent, we all live in a constant state of frenzy, doing everything and nothing at the same time. It's like we are desperately
trying to go north and south at the same time, wondering why after
all this effort and energy we are still in the same place. *Frenzy* is the
desperate state of constant unfocused effort and random behavior
that consistently fails to produce desired results. Frenzy is not just
the dreaded treadmill to nowhere. When work and life feel like a
treadmill and we are on autopilot, at least we know it. We can see
ourselves doing the same ole thing day in and day out. But frenzy is
entirely different than being on a treadmill because most of us don't
even realize frenzy is in our lives. We feel frenzy, but can't see it
because we all have an addiction to being overwhelmed with things
to do. This is what I call an addiction to frenzy.

To some extent, we all have an addiction to frenzy, and much
like any compulsive disease, it's invisible to us, threatens our well-
being, and makes our lives miserable. Our addiction to frenzy is
based on an insatiable need that fills our lives with tasks and things
to do, which never allows us to slow down enough to focus on what
really matters. Some of the time, our addiction is the result of some
unresolved or unfulfilled need we have to matter or to belong. For
example, imagine connecting with a friend you haven't seen in a long
time. Let's say you run into them at a store, or you decided to connect
with them over coffee to catch up on life. Your conversation is likely
to sound a little like this:

> **Friend:** *Hey gurl, how have things been going for you? It's been
> a while since we connected.*

**You:** *Things have been good but really busy. My job has me going to multiple meetings every day, and I'm up for promotion so I have to attend team meetings to stay up to date. My kids are doing well, Charles (my ten-year-old son) is playing soccer, so I'm always either picking him up or dropping him off, and Senay (my seven-year-old girl) just started a STEM after-school program and she loves it. So my husband, Marquees, and I are swamped with getting supplies for her projects. On top of that, I'm heading up my church's fundraising committee, and we have so much to do, I'm always on the phone problem solving and swamped with meetings. Did I tell you that I'm also going back to school to finish my degree? So a few nights a week I'm in class and cramming for the next test. I'm just so busy all the time.*

**Friend:** *Wow, sounds like you have a lot going on. I'm also super busy. I'm teaching at three community colleges now because I can use the extra money and they all pay really good. My kids are also doing well, and James (my seventeen-year-old) is applying for college, and every night we are researching colleges that fit him. I also completed my real estate license last year and sold three homes! Things are going great, but my schedule is always packed between showing homes and preparing for classes.*

The conversation is sometimes defined by saying, "I'm so busy, isn't that great?" Think about it: what we are really saying is that I matter because I'm busy. Imagine for a moment what we would think about someone who said, "I'm really not busy at all these days, and most of the time is filled with things I really enjoy." We might think wow, what a slacker, they really aren't hustling to get ahead. Truth is, our addiction to frenzy doesn't just happen overnight; it's a slow process that occurs over time until, well . . . we break down.

My own addiction to frenzy occurred when I was in graduate school at UC Berkeley. During that time, I also had a full-time job with Upward Bound in a city that was an hour away, which required a grueling daily commute that began at 6:00 A.M. On top of that, I along with a few friends had embarked on launching a nonprofit agency focused on leadership and healing Black young people in Oakland, California, and our work was growing. I had just hired three staff, which meant that I was involved with constant fundraising to assure that I could make payroll. Nedra and I were brand-new parents learning to care for our first-born son, Takai, who was an incredibly colicky child, which meant that we hadn't slept well in months. Oh yeah, did I say that I was facing a deadline at UC Berkeley to finish my research and complete my dissertation? The cherry on top was that we had found a new place to live and rent was pushing the limit of our income, so the pressure to keep going and grinding it out was real.

One night, after getting my son to sleep, my mind, spirit, and body broke down. I didn't know what was happening at first. My heart was racing, but my mind was saying, "Everything is OK," then out of nowhere, a wave of emotion overwhelmed me and literally brought me to my knees in tears. I hadn't cried like that in years. Nedra heard me and asked me what was going on, and all I could get out was, "It's too much, I'm not sure I can take it." I had rationalized my stress by calling it "getting my hustle on," but it was much more than that. It was my first, but not last, encounter with my own addiction to frenzy.

## THE CULT OF TO-DO LISTS

Raise your hand if you have a to-do list! Don't just nod your head in silent agreement as you read this . . . raise your hand with honest pride. We all, to some extent, are guided by our to-do lists because these simple tools help keep all the mundane stuff in our heads in order. To-do lists allow us to increase daily or monthly productivity without having to memorize and feel overwhelmed by all the things that need to be accomplished. But a to-do list is much deeper than that. It's really a symbol of modern capitalist culture that guides our daily behaviors.

We are all built with a disconnect between our conscious and unconscious minds. Our conscious mind organizes, categorizes, and prioritizes tasks, but when these tasks are not completed, the unconscious mind gets annoyed and sends a message to the conscious mind that something is unfinished. That message then sparks the conscious mind to recall what hasn't been completed. It's a nagging feeling when we have unfinished tasks dangling around. That's why when we literally scratch off a task from our list, we feel better and more in control of things.

To-do lists aren't bad in themselves; they are just symbols of how capitalist culture permeates nearly all aspects of our lives. Capitalist culture is the values and core beliefs about how our economy and society should be organized. Values like individualism, privatization, unregulated profits, productivity, and competition permeate our daily lives. Researchers have argued that these values can be detrimental to well-being and can harm our own mental health.[1] This is largely because these values tend to determine the value of human beings based on what a person can produce or earn. This is why we admire and celebrate wealthy people. Of course this all operates at our subconscious level, and most of the time we don't even realize it.

One of the most dangerous consequences of capitalist culture is the deep sense of emptiness, isolation, and inadequacy it creates among all of us. For example, during the 2020 pandemic when millions of small businesses were forced to close and entire industries were shut down, millions of families lost their jobs and income. Families were unable to keep food on the table and pay rent or their mortgages. Despite the fact that the pandemic created the most severe economic collapse in history, researchers reported increased depression, anxiety, and shame among Americans because they needed government assistance to survive. This is largely because we define ourselves by our work, and our value is determined by our employment. Productivity, and the value we find in being productive, is just the natural by-product of capitalist culture. So to-do lists aren't bad—we just have to keep in mind the real consequences of defining and valuing ourselves by scratching off those pesky items on our lists. Our intense desire for productivity, while necessary at times, can get out of control. This is how we slip into an addiction to frenzy without even knowing it. We digest large doses of capitalist culture without the awareness of what these values are doing to our physical health, mental well-being, and the quality of our relationships. The only way to pivot away from our addiction to frenzy is to first recognize the impact frenzy has on our joy, meaning, and human connectedness.

\* \* \*

In an instant, my priority had changed from getting funding for my organization to getting my son out of the locked car. Takai must have seen the terror on my face because I frantically and desperately tried to get him to squirm out of his car seat and pull the door latch, but then of course he was only a year old, and that wasn't going to happen. So he started to cry because I wasn't able to get to him and he could sense that I was afraid. Then something inside of me said STOP, PAUSE, and BREATHE. I had to slow down in order to move forward. On the sidewalk near my car, I noticed a phone booth where a thick Yellow Pages book dangled from a cable (we didn't really have cell phones back then). I could see my car from the phone booth, so I quickly ran to the phone booth, grabbed the remaining quarters in my pocket, and called a locksmith to open the car door. Brooks Towing was only a few blocks away, so I called them first. STOP, PAUSE, and BREATHE . . . A woman answered, I explained what happened, and she said that someone would be there in ten minutes! It actually took about an hour. After the locksmith pulled up, it was all over in less than a minute. He pulled out his handy Slim Jim, gently slid it down between the rubber seal on the door and the window, and jiggled and pulled, jiggled and pulled, and then pop, the door lock opened! I grabbed my son, embraced him, and squeezed him so tight I could still smell the baby oil on his neck. Then we made a pact never to tell Nedra about the incident. Needless to say, I missed the meeting and never received the funding, but it was all good because I had learned a valuable lesson about the impact of frenzy.

## WHAT IS FLOW?

*Flow* is the state of consistent, focused, and nearly effortless activity that consistently produces desired results. Flow is the state of awareness that is free of judgment, doubt, fear, and confusion and is guided by a sense of effortless certainty. Researchers Jacob Getzels and Mihaly Csikszentmihalyi first studied flow in the '60s when watching artists at work. They were intrigued by the artists' persistence and intense focus during painting without becoming tired or hungry. Later Csikszentmihalyi expanded on this research and explored flow during work, play, and other activities.

You have probably experienced flow before. If you have ever been immersed in an activity with sharp concentration and with your skills being used almost effortlessly to reach the goal or solution, you are so focused that you lose track of time, and your self-awareness drops away. That's what researchers describe as flow, when attention is totally keyed to the activity itself. When this happens, researchers claim, your mind becomes so focused and absorbed in the activity that you "forget yourself" and begin to act effortlessly, with a heightened sense of awareness of the here and now. Athletes often describe this as "being in the zone."[2] This also happens in social settings when we work and play in groups, like when sports teams, sales teams, and design teams work together to creatively solve problems.

Flow is actually a concept that has been practiced for thousands of years and is found in Taoist writing as practicing "The Way," or in Confucianism principles based in prudence, attention to detail, balance, and inter-connectedness with others. In African and Indigenous cultures that promote social harmony and values or behaviors that achieve it, flow is found not so much in an individual person accomplishing a challenging task, but in the harmony of groups of people effortlessly working together.

## FLOW AND JUSTICE

Flow occurs not in the absence of obstacles but because of them. Take for instance a river flowing down a hill; water will flow around a large rock just as easily as a fallen tree. No matter what the obstacle, water will effortlessly seek its inevitable path of least resistance. Our capacity to flow in our efforts to advance justice works in the same way. Power and effectiveness are often the result of finding our flow toward justice. You may be familiar with Howard Thurman's quote "Don't ask yourself what the world needs. Ask yourself what makes you come alive, and go do that, because what the world needs is people who have come alive." Thurman makes an important point about the relationship between flow and justice because he is showing us the relationship between social change and personal transformation. The more we practice flow, the greater possibility there is for social change. This may seem counterintuitive because there are urgent, pressing issues that harm communities and cause unjust suffering to precious families. You may be saying that there's critical work to do now that requires immediate and swift action. This is true, but if we are not aware of our frenzied work for justice, we might believe that we are building a new house when actually we are just putting out the fire in one.

Social change always requires three types of actors—firefighters, builders, and architects—and each requires elements of flow to create a more fair and just society. Firefighters are the first responders who do the important work that addresses harm and injustice in our institutions. These are organizers who support families with fighting unfair housing policies, social workers who support youth with challenges in school, and youth-development professionals who create after-school opportunities for learning and growth. Firefighters respond to the injustices in society that sometimes are invisible. Firefighters need flow to avoid burnout, unproductive stress, fatigue, and depression. Without flow, "the state of awareness that is free of judgment, doubt, fear, and confusion and is guided by a sense of effortless certainty," firefighters can lose focus and slip into frenzy.

Builders, on the other hand, are those social change actors who construct alternative institutions, policies, and laws that are fair and inclusive. Builders are parents who work tirelessly to raise healthy children in challenging neighborhoods; they are also social entrepreneurs who create organizations and businesses that advance our society toward inclusion and fairness. Builders are those who work in the nonprofit organizations, government agencies, and socially responsible businesses directed toward creating a more just world. Builders need flow to take a step back from time to time and ask if they are building the right thing. Again, builders run the risk of slipping into frenzy and can spend years trying to build an organization, business, or agency that falls down the slippery slope of chasing dollars because its work attracts capital or will receive funding. Flow allows for builders to reflect on the question "Am I building the right thing?"

Architects need firefighters and builders, and no social change would be possible without all three. Architects generally take a bird's-eye view of things and have the opportunity to learn from folks on the frontlines, gain knowledge from studying the issue, and produce a set of ideas that integrate both. Architects are people like Patrisse Cullors, Alicia Garza, and Opal Tometi who felt the pain of Black dehumanization and sparked the largest movement for Black dignity in the twenty-first century. (I'd like to add that Alicia was formerly my graduate student. Sup, Alicia!) Without flow, architects in the frenzy of work may lose sight of what is important for justice and become detached from how people feel and experience daily life. Remember, flow is an awareness that is free of judgment, doubt, fear, and confusion and is guided by a sense of effortless certainty. So when Cullors, Garza, and Tometi used the hashtag #BlackLivesMatter, they did so free of judgment, doubt, fear, and confusion about Black humanity, and they were guided by a sense of effortless certainty about the need to highlight the injustice of George Zimmerman's acquittal while at the same time lift up Black humanity.

Flow is an important ingredient in our work for racial and social justice, and we all need to find it. In our work for justice and our passion to confront white supremacy, sexism, homophobia, and so on, we have in some ways created a martyr culture where people are celebrated and lifted up for "putting it all on the line." Martyr culture is dangerous because we forget what it costs us, which is our families, friends, health, and well-being. I know that I've used the phrase "she is a soldier" or "she's down" when I wanted to convey the idea that someone is passionate about justice and freedom. The idea of tireless dedication, relentless struggle, and gritty determination for justice is of course celebrated among progressives. But how often do we think about the consequences of "being down" on our collective well-being?

Many of us were devastated when we learned that the powerful and passionate activist Erica Garner, the late Eric Garner's daughter, unexpectedly died from a heart attack at twenty-seven in December 2017. Almost verbatim, many activists say that the issues and challenges (poverty, violence, substances, joblessness, poor education) have taken a toll on their well-being, and yet the solutions they have just do not go deep enough.[3] Creating and sustaining social justice movements require intense dedication and commitment that often leads to burnout, which in turn fosters loss of purpose. Activist Yashna Maya Padamsee commented, "We put our bodies on the line everyday—because we care so deeply about our work—hunger strikes, long marches, long days at the computer, or long days organizing on a street corner, or a public bus, or a congregation. Skip a meal, keep working. Don't sleep, keep working. Our communities are still suffering, so I must keep going."[4] Theologian Thomas Merton put it best when he said:

> There is a pervasive form of contemporary violence to which the idealist most easily succumbs: activism and overwork. The rush and pressure of modern life are a form, perhaps the most common form, of its innate violence. To allow oneself to be carried away by a multitude of conflicting concerns, to surrender to too many demands, to commit oneself to too many projects, to want to help everyone in everything, is to succumb to violence. The frenzy of our activism neutralizes our work for peace. It

*destroys our own inner capacity for peace. It destroys the fruit-*
*fulness of our own work, because it kills the root of inner wisdom*
*which makes work fruitful.*[5]

Flow is a critical ingredient for social change because it gives us
the permission to separate from the madness of capitalist culture and
tap into the ancient power of slowing down. This is why Chicana the-
orist Gloria E. Anzaldúa's work is so important in cultivating what
she calls "spiritual activism," a worldview that centers Indigenous,
African, and Eastern practices that offer grounding, purpose, and
flow. Anzaldúa reminds us that real power is not only built from
mass mobilization or control of electoral politics, but rather from our
collective capacity to detach, even for a moment, from the frenzy of
life. Capitalist culture will tell us that we don't have time, there's so
much urgency, and slowing down is a sign of weakness. But in truth
when we unplug from frenzy, we pivot to a more sustainable form of
deep change. Flow comes from the consciousness resulting from sustained enjoyment and effortless focus on goodness. Flow is pure, and
if you've ever danced, painted, written a poem, delivered a speech,
played a musical instrument, sung a song, or simply watched the
sunset, congratulations, you know how to create flow in your life and
work. If you are like me, you may need more support and permission
to find flow in your work and in your life. Here are a few ways to
begin your "flow practice" that you might find awkward, but once
you get the hang of it, all of us working collectively to create a better
world will benefit.

First, take an inventory of your activities over a typical week.
You might list activities like took bus to work, did grocery shopping,
prepared for meeting, took children to park, sent emails to team.
Once you have a list of twenty to thirty activities, jot next to each
activity a number from 1 to 5, 1 being a miserable activity and 5
being an extremely enjoyable one. Next, take a look at how many
5s you have next to activities, how many 4s, how many 3s, and so
on. The purpose of this practice is to simply become aware of frenzy
in your life. Chances are that if you have more 1s and 2s next to
these activities, you're in frenzy. The goal is to not just eliminate

less-enjoyable activities, but rather to become aware of these activities and how they might contribute to frenzy. You might ask, What do these activities feel like? What do they do to my well-being? How do these activities impact my family and friends?

Second, create opportunities to rupture connections to frenzy. I know this is difficult when we have to work two jobs, make sure our kids do their homework, care for aging parents, and deal with an unsupportive partner. Truth is, flow isn't always easy to create, but we need to find small windows of opportunity to exhale and flow. Burn a candle when you're reading at night, take five minutes to meditate in the morning, try to increase the time you spend on things you enjoy even if it's just five minutes a day. Don't beat yourself up if you can't do it for an hour a day, because when you develop five-minute micro-habits, they can grow into larger habits. Schedule your "flow practice" time, and let others know that this is not just self-care but rather part of our collective movement-building work. Over time, this shifts the expectation that grinding it out is what should be expected of social change leaders.

Third, at work, rather than ask if something can be completed sooner (often with an unrealistic timeline), ask how something can be completed with deeper meaning, purpose, and intentionality, which sometimes is overlooked when we are in frenzy. Negotiate your deadlines and timelines in ways that keep things moving but create the space for you to "sit with" ideas, focus on the process, and think through solutions. Great ideas come when you are in flow, not frenzy.

Integrating flow in our work and lives is a key step in our final pivot. Just asking how we might cultivate flow in our work and in our lives will create the space we all need to reimagine social change. Remember, justice and freedom are not just the absence of oppression, but rather they're the ability to truly create the type of world we envision. Somewhere along the way, we've picked up all the bad habits that come with capitalist culture, and we forgot to question new ways of being with each other. So at work and in our lives, let's ask, How do we cultivate more flow? Because when we ask the question, we will ultimately find the answer each of us needs for deep change.

# 11

# *Rest*

During the 1970s there were only eight television channels, and two of them were dedicated to cartoons on Saturday mornings until noon. So after eating my grits (salt and pepper, no sugar), I would head to the living room with my brothers and fight over which cartoons we would watch. First, we'd watch Gumby and Pokey, a series of adventures of a green animated clay boy and his faithful sidekick Pokey, a small red clay pony. Gumby and Pokey would take my brothers and me on the coolest adventures an eleven-year-old could imagine. One Saturday morning we were introduced to "The Tortoise and the Hare." Most of us are familiar with the story: A hare brags and boasts about his own speed and teases a tortoise about how slow he is. The hare challenges the tortoise to a race, and the tortoise declines. Unsatisfied, the hare continues to encourage the tortoise to race him, and finally the tortoise agrees. They meet at the starting line, and the race ensues. The hare, being much faster than the tortoise, speeds off and takes a huge lead. Confident that his significant lead will guarantee his victory, he decides to take a nap under a nearby tree. Slowly, the tortoise continues his steady pace and passes the sleeping hare. When the hare wakes up refreshed and ready to go, he notices the tortoise is near the finish line. The hare runs as fast as he can, but it's too late—the tortoise has already won. The story is one of Aesop's Fables and conveys two important lessons. The first is that consistency and commitment over time pay off. The second is that if you are tired and take time to rest, you're always gonna lose.

We have an ongoing war with rest in our society, and it's killing us. There are so many messages in our culture about the wastefulness of rest, which get reinforced in our language and fortified by our behavior. Ideas about rest as a sign of weakness begin at an early age in cartoons and in fables like "The Tortoise and the Hare." It's no wonder that research shows that by age eight, children have already developed dysfunctional attitudes toward sleep and rest.[1] There are so many messages in our society telling us rest is a sign of weakness that we sometimes can't even see these messages. Take for instance the Folgers coffee slogan, "The best part of waking up is Folgers in your cup." Now, I love my coffee in the morning, and I'm not saying that drinking coffee is all bad. The point is that coffee culture is really about the consumption of caffeine, a stimulant to keep us sharp, awake, and more productive. Starbucks is not successful because of its delicious coffee but because it has learned to exploit the idea that rest is weakness, because we all consume caffeine to help us stay productive and awake. Imagine the alternative: a multi-billion-dollar company with stores on every street corner, where you can easily walk in, buy a cup of a warm beverage to become sleepy, and then snuggle up for a nap!

We also see this message in popular culture. Take for instance the following lines from a few popular hip-hop lyrics:

- ► "I never sleep, cause sleep is the cousin of death" (Nas)

- ► "I don't sleep" (Lil Wayne)

- ► "Run the streets all day, I can sleep when I die" (Young Jeezy)

The phrase *rest in peace* is typically reserved for funerals—the sanctity of rest is granted only in death. The message we receive about rest as weakness is everywhere, and every day we unconsciously take small bites of this poisonous message without knowing it. The idea that rest is weakness is also true for those of us who have dedicated our lives to justice, freedom, and equality. Consider the popular lyrics in Sweet Honey in the Rock's "Ella's Song," "We who believe in freedom cannot rest." On the surface, phrases like this mean that we must remain committed and dedicated in our tireless work for freedom. But on a deeper level, it reinforces the same message as "The Tortoise and the Hare": if you rest, you will lose. As I mentioned in the last chapter, if we are unaware of the ways that we create and celebrate martyr culture, we run the risk of burning out, creating unsustainable lifestyles, and damaging our relationships.

These ideas about sleep are made even worse when we are bombarded with messages that work, not leisure, nor rest, should occupy most of our time. Arianna Huffington calls attention to what she calls a "sleep crisis" in her book *The Sleep Revolution*. "The unquestioning belief that work should always have the top claim on our time has been a costly one. And it has gotten worse as technology has allowed a growing number of us to carry our work with us in our pockets and purses in the form of phones—wherever we go."[2] How many minutes out of every day do you have to literally get up and walk to get your phone? If you are like me, and millions of other people, probably zero minutes because our phones are always with us, or next to our beds, with work, tasks, and reminders comfortably waiting for us to obey. The phone has become like a third arm, attached to our bodies, and when it's missing, it aches.

## REST IS FOR THE WEAK!

One of the most underestimated challenges to justice is rest. Rest is not just sleep, meaningless hibernation, inactive slumber, or useless dormancy. Rest is an act of freedom, a middle finger to oppression that tells us to obey its command to work tirelessly for the pleasure of capitalism. I know that may sound like a strong statement, but let me explain.

The idea that rest is weakness has a long history in America, and it is still deeply rooted in white supremacist Western culture. Horatio Alger stories that emphasize self-determination combined with the Protestant work ethic, which promoted the idea that hard work made people more likely to go to heaven, together helped lay the ideological groundwork that devalued rest. The idea that capitalism will reward your hard work was deeply engrained in the American belief system and fueled by the Industrial Revolution. If America was built by the Industrial Revolution, then the Industrial Revolution was built on African slave labor. This means that enslaved Africans were primarily and singularly seen as labor, the magic cog in the industrial capitalist machine that could produce the raw materials for the new industrial economy. OK, enough history, but basically Black bodies were and continue to be viewed through the lens of labor. Despite 400 years of free labor in sugarcane fields in the Caribbean and cotton or tobacco plantations in the South, the ridiculous term *lazy* is still hurled at Blacks and other communities of color. *Lazy* is used to justify the sanctity of capitalism and serves as evidence as to why Black folks as a whole haven't yet benefited from capitalism, because they haven't worked hard enough.

African slave labor is just one of many examples of how the idea of rest as weakness permeates our society. This also applies to Mexican farmworkers in the Central Valley of California and the Chinese people whose labor created the intercontinental rail system. People of color, in the minds of white America, have primarily been seen as labor to exploit. Rest and leisure are reserved for the white folk, who supposedly *earned* the luxury to rest. Rest and race are intertwined and boil down to who has the right to rest, and under what conditions should rest and leisure be granted, and who has earned the ability to rest without stigma or ridicule. Rest for folks of color, in white supremacist culture, has to be earned first by demonstrating unquestioned loyalty and dedication to work, sweat, and toil. Only then, after you cannot work to maximum output, is rest considered permissible. Even then, rest is viewed as a way to "recharge" only to plug back into the frenzy and hustle of work.

BIPOC women are particularly susceptible to the idea of rest as weakness and are overworked, undervalued, and under pressure. Terrie Williams put it best when she said in her book *Black Pain: It Just Looks Like We're Not Hurting*:

> *I have come to believe that as Black women our threshold for pain is too high. We have embraced very destructive beliefs about our ability to "handle it all" . . . our ability to put ourselves aside as we tend to the needs of our employers, partners, children, family—everyone but ourselves! . . . Working 24/7 is a primary symptom of depression for Black women . . . I was the one who was always worried about whether other people were over their limit, stressed, or overworked. But when it came to myself, I had no mercy. I would work until I dropped, meet unreasonable deadlines, sacrifice weekend days at the office, and generally push myself beyond normal endurance. I felt the sacrifices I needed to make in the interest of my business, clients, family, and others were more important than my needs.*[3]

I know that this is a daily struggle for Nedra. Only recently, and after a few really good therapy sessions, did we both come to the realization that she would just take care of . . . well . . . pretty much everything. She took care of anything dealing with our children, organized her friends' birthday parties, made arrangements for her father's medical care, supervised three employees, and made sure that we had groceries in the house. She did laundry, coordinated meetings, organized fundraisers, and made sure to send old friends holiday cards every year. We both made a commitment to give ourselves permission to rest and take time to do things we enjoyed together. I remember the first week we tried it, she slept in until about 8:30 A.M. for a few days. I must have said something unsupportive to her about waking up so late because she said to me, "You judge me for working too hard, and now you are judging me for sleeping late and resting." I'm just as guilty as anyone for thinking that rest is for the weak.

The idea that rest is weakness shows up differently for Black men. We call it "getting our hustle on" or "grinding," and it's disguised as a necessary evil to deal with the fact that Black men are last hired, first fired, and locked out of many employment opportunities. Folks gotta eat and pay rent, despite the fact that they face racism in employment. Hustling or grinding is a way to survive and put money in your pocket. Black men have always found innovative ways to put food on the table. The thing about hustling is that it devalues rest and places a premium on work. Hustling is reinforced by the idea that we need to endure stress and is fortified by toxic masculinity.

I remember reading a piece in the *New York Times* titled "I Pray for Murder (Sometimes): I've Learned How to Dodge a Bullet. But How Do You Dodge a Stroke?" It's a brilliant essay by Damon Young, who recounts his teenage years growing comfortable with violence and learning when and how to avoid potentially dangerous violence in his neighborhood. In his thirties he realized that many of his friends who had learned to survive violence from their earlier years were dying of strokes, heart disease, and high blood pressure.

> *I've learned to associate black maleness with early death. And because I'm so familiar with the possibility of violence, I've convinced myself that I can avert it. I can sense when the stillness of the street is a precursor to danger, like the moment before a storm hits and the air adopts a menacing tranquility. I know the shuffle of someone carrying them tools in baggy jeans. I can feel it when the clamor at a nightclub shifts from festive to menacing. I know how to run. I know how to sit in public spaces (with my back facing a wall, so that I can see everything). I know how to park in lots (with the back in first, to make a quick getaway if necessary). I know how to look like I know how to fight.*
>
> *But how do you duck from a stroke? How do you run when cancer decides to chase you? How do you mean-mug a blood*

*clot? . . . the same ecosystem of susceptibilities that heightens*
*the risk of violent death at 17 just transfers that risk inside our*
*adult bodies. We age out of bullets and into high blood pressure.*[4]

Rest is not just the ability to get a good night's sleep; it's also the ability to not worry and have sustained peace of mind. These things usually come from the stability of a good job, knowing that your children are safe, and that you're not going to lose your home. These things are not always available if you're poor, an immigrant, or young and Black. Young's comments remind us that the lack of rest can be deadly and is yet another type of violence that often goes undetected for BIPOC folks. The stress that comes from worry, concern over safety, and the persistent cuts from racial microaggressions all adds up and creates yet another form of inequality we rarely talk about and vaguely understand—inequality in our rest.

## REST INEQUALITY

*Rest inequality* is the gap in the quality, duration, and amount of rest we get. It is created and maintained by structural inequality and is not simply the result of personal choice as some would have you believe. Researchers have found that the duration, quality, and frequency of rest in general and sleep in particular are shaped by income level, housing conditions, employment status, type of work, and race. Dr. Dayna Johnson, Emory University public health researcher, has extensively studied sleep disparities and has shown "that racial/ethnic minorities are more likely to experience, for instance, shorter sleep durations, less deep sleep, inconsistent sleep timing, and lower sleep continuity in comparison to Whites."[5] Sleep is one of the important aspects of rest, and more and more people are paying attention to the importance of sleep for learning, mental health, stress reduction, and other forms of physical health. There is consensus among researchers that a significant "sleep disparity" exists in America, with African American and Latino groups overall having poorer sleep quality than whites.

In the June 2015 issue of the journal *Sleep* researchers published a study on the sleep quality of Black, white, Chinese, and Hispanic adults in six cities across the United States. The study involved more than 6,000 people in order to better understand the impact of geography and race on sleep and its impact on health outcomes. The participants wore Fitbit-like bracelets that could track their sleep. The researchers found that African Americans in the group were getting the least amount of sleep among the racial groups. On average, the sleep quality of whites was superior to that of the other ethnic groups.[6]

Rest inequality is not only about the racial and ethnic gaps in the quality and duration of our sleep. But rest inequality also involves how we spend our leisure time, the quality of how we play, the quality of our recreation, how much we worry, and the amount of time doing pleasurable activities. For example, researchers have found that, when compared to whites, racial and ethnic minority groups are less likely to engage in leisure time.[7] Leisure time involves activities that are not related to work or household duties. Leisure might include taking a walk, dancing, gardening, sewing, or physical exercise like jogging or bike riding.

The worst thing about rest inequality is that some of us refuse to believe it's a problem at all. Some might ask, "There are so many important forms of inequality in our society—how can sleep be just as significant as health inequality, educational inequality, or income inequality?" All these issues are significant and important, and we need to continue to address these disparities. Rest inequality in many ways forces us to see the connections between all forms of inequality. You can't eliminate rest inequality without addressing income inequality because they are interdependent and intertwined. For example, if you work multiple jobs to make ends meet, you have less time to rest because you work more. Working more may eliminate or make it difficult to find time to rest. Sleep inequality permeates all aspects of our lives and requires that we rethink, reimagine, and readjust our connection to how we work, live, and play. So as an act of resistance and a collective movement to end rest inequality, let's all take a nap in the middle of the day without feeling guilty—and post it on Instagram! Reclaim your rest!

Some countries don't experience rest inequality like we do in the United States. There is a lot to be learned from places like Spain, where rest is an important part of the culture. The *siesta* in Spain is a time of day between 3:00 and 5:00 P.M. when stores, banks, and public museums shut down for a couple hours so that people can rest. Spaniards usually go home for a nap, spend time with friends and family, and just slow down. This practice is actually common in places with hot climates. Countries like Nigeria, Costa Rica, and Ecuador have similar practices of resting during the day. Some countries have taken the idea of rest inequality so seriously that it guides the country's domestic policy. In the West, we look to our economy to indicate how well our country is doing without consideration of the labor and lack of rest the economy requires. Gross domestic product (GDP) is an economic indicator we use to measure the strength and health of our nation. In 1970 Bhutan flipped the script from GDP and redefined the metrics for a strong and prosperous country by introducing Gross National Happiness, an annual index that measures elements of the nation's quality of life and happiness. Bhutan regularly conducts a national survey across nine domains that contribute to a person's happiness. These include living standards, health (both physical and mental health, how much time is spent on work and non-work, sleep, and work-life balance), psychological well-being, education, quality of life, life satisfaction, and spirituality. There are eighty-seven questions assessing different domains of rest including leisure time, time spent sleeping, sleep quality, loss of sleep due to worry, and overall life satisfaction. Bhutan understands that rest is justice. . . !

## THE FATALISTIC GRIND FOR JUSTICE

I hope more than anything else that you will take stock of your own rest habits and reflect on your belief systems about rest. Think about what's happening with your own sleep—how much rest do you get every day? How do you spend your leisure time? How often do you lose sleep and rest due to worry and stress? I know from my own work with foundation executives, community leaders, organizers, and students that there exists a "grind culture" in our work to improve our society. This grind culture permeates how we relate to one another and places a premium on getting the job done even if it means working through the night, missing your children's soccer game, or postponing a night out with your friends.

As a professor, I have supported numerous students with breaking their addiction to grind culture. I recall one student who was building her own nonprofit organization that worked in underperforming schools. She also was organizing parents to reject the district's proposal to close several schools in the city, and it required an enormous amount of work. In the graduate seminar I was teaching, she had asked for several extensions for papers that were due because her plate was full. When she came into my office, she looked tired. Not tired like she had a long day, but exhausted tired like she was holding on to a sack of bricks that was pulling her down to the bottom of the sea. She explained to me that on top of all that she was doing, her mother was sick and she was the primary caregiver. Despite all that was going on, she still believed that she had to grind it out for the community. I explained to her, as I do to all my students, that nothing is more important than your health and well-being. I suggested that she take some time off and get someone else to take over some of her activities. We talked for over an hour, and she explained to me that she just couldn't imagine what people would think of her if she stepped aside, and she didn't want to let the community down. About a week or two later I noticed that she hadn't returned to class, and I learned that she had been hospitalized after passing out from exhaustion. The following semester she came to see me, and we talked about what happened. She looked so much better, her eyes were alive, and I could tell she was feeling better. She explained to me that being hospitalized was one of the best things that could have happened to her because she was forced to rest. She also took the time to reprioritize her life and began riding her bike again for exercise.

Grind culture is dangerous, and we have to learn how to rethink our deeply engrained fatalistic ideas about how to engage in community change. We also have to build a practice where we prioritize rest, not as an act of self-indulgence or self-care, but rather as a critical component of our journey toward justice. This is why we have to understand rest as a right, not a privilege for those who can get and enjoy it.

## THE RIGHT TO REPLENISH

A good example of the necessity of rest can be seen in nature. I'm not a farmer, but my father would explain to me that crops that are grown in the same soil over time can actually be harmful to the soil. This is because overproduction of crops in the same soil drains the soil of key nutrients necessary for growth and flourishing. The soil is the most important factor in growing healthy plants, and without good soil nothing you do really matters. Pops explained that wise farmers let the soil rest for a season, knowing that resting the soil will ultimately produce better crops. Resting the soil regenerates nutrients, replenishes important minerals, and restores soil quality.

We should learn from these wise farmers and prioritize the need for us to replenish. We all have a right to restore ourselves, and rest can be an act of justice! When we rest and restore, we call attention to the oppressive ways that capitalist culture devalues rest and tells us that rest is reserved only for those who have earned it. We need to democratize rest and make it more available to those that need it most. This means rethinking the hours we spend at work (it's time to rethink the forty-hour work week) and reimagining how and where we work. The COVID-19 pandemic forced us all to rethink these issues simply because some of us had to work from home. This required companies to create new ways of working for their employees. How do we exercise our right to rest? Here are a few ways to pivot from thinking about rest as weakness to practicing our right to rest.

First, ask yourself, "What is my relationship to rest?" This question forces you to identify the messages you hold about rest and identify the consequences these messages have for you. Do you think that rest is not important or takes time away from more important activities? Where did you learn these messages? Do you get enough rest? How do you rest? What is your favorite type of rest? What was the worst rest you ever had? What gets in the way of your rest? These are just a few questions that can help you identify your relationship with rest. Take some time to write in a journal your responses to these questions to better identify your relationship to rest. This is an important step because by asking these questions, we can also better understand the structural impediments or opportunities that shape our rest habits. A lot of us assume that when we go to sleep at night, a pillow and time are enough to achieve rest. But these questions allow us to go a little deeper. Once we do that, we can actually see and name our relationship to rest.

Second, take an inventory of your rest habits. I asked earlier in this chapter how many minutes in a day you spend getting up and walking to get your cell phone. When the phone is near your bed charging up, it might also be draining you of your rest. This is because our brains are looking for that next beep when an email arrives or the vibration buzz to notify you when someone comments on your IG post. These little things (all results of capitalist culture) all impact our rest. Take some time to make a list of how you rest over the period of a week. Begin with how you felt waking up in the morning, and list what you did during the day that you considered restful. Did you exercise or go to the farmers market? Did you respond to emails and crank out the report that you've been avoiding? Just list a few activities that either enhanced or impaired your rest during the week. Once you have this list, you can explore ways to reduce or eliminate those activities that impaired your rest and try to add things that enhance your rest quality. Basically by doing this you are creating your own rest plan and reprioritizing ways to enhance the frequency, quality, and duration of your rest activities.

Third, form a "radical rest" group of colleagues at work or among your friends. A radical rest group is just five to ten people who are curious about the significance of rest in our efforts for social change. Now, I know it sounds like a support group for rest, but it's not. A radical rest group meets regularly—once a month, just like a book club—to discuss how to build systems of support for rest. Remember rest inequality is not just a personal choice but rather a result of structural inequality and cultural beliefs. A radical rest group comes together to reimagine how to democratize rest in our society. How can we reshape policies in workplace settings to give employees more time to rest? How might we reimagine the work week in order to provide more time to spend with friends and family? How might we cultivate a culture where rest is viewed not as a weakness but as a strength?

Everyone has the right to rest, and it is an important step in our pivot from frenzy addiction to flow. Rest is like food, and just like with food deserts in our cities and neighborhoods, we need to pay attention to how we are cultivating and replenishing our soil. Just like the wise farmers who allow their land to rest, or the hare who rested under the tree, replenishing ourselves is the only real way to make the deep change we need in our world. So go take a nap!

# 12

Wild

*And Max sailed back over a year, and in and out of
weeks, and through a day and into the night . . . and
when he came to the place where the wild things are they
roared their terrible roars and gnashed their terrible
teeth, and rolled their terrible eyes and showed their terrible claws till Max said "BE STILL" and tamed them.*

MAURICE SENDAK, *Where the Wild Things Are*

When I think about the wilderness, I imagine lots of trees
and vast swaths of mountains and rivers. When I was in
my twenties I traveled to Ghana in West Africa and visited
Kakum National Park with a group and walked across a wooden
bridge suspended over a deep rain forest. The bridge was held
together only by wooden plank slats and rope. When I was cross-
ing the rickety bridge, I stopped and gazed with amazement into
the vast rain forest where the trees only ended with the horizon.
Below we could hear a cacophony of animals and insects. Our guide
explained to us that the reason we walk *above* the forest is because

it's entirely too dangerous to walk *through* the forest by foot. "There are a lot of things that could harm you down there. There are poisonous bugs, monkeys, snakes, and even brushing against the wrong plant might kill you," he explained. Our guide knew the park like it was his own backyard and had spent many days and nights exploring the terrain. He boasted about how he could spend more than a month in that wilderness and come back unscathed. "There are rules you have to follow when you are in the wild, and if you don't follow the rules, you won't survive . . . nature is so unforgiving," he exclaimed with pride.

Unlike the wilderness I experienced in my twenties, today's wilderness is much more complex yet equally as dangerous. Today's wilderness is not simply defined by dark forests with dangerous beasts but rather by its thick uncertainty and deep fear. Climate change, poverty, sexism, racism, homophobia, and transphobia are just a few of the complex and dangerous issues that we have to confront— our wilderness. I hope this book has provided you with guidelines through your journey, just like our tour guide offered us in Kakum park. We all need guidelines to help us navigate the complex and dangerous wilderness we find ourselves in as we boldly hike into an uncertain and unpredictable frontier of social transformation. The pivots in this book are like guideposts in our journey through the wild; if we follow them, they will allow us to make better decisions, see our destination more clearly, and help us finally see that we really were never in the wilderness at all.

## BEING STILL IN THE WILD

*Wilderness* is a perspective that we hold about things we view as unknown, untamed, and uncontrollable. Some people are really comfortable in the wilderness, while others find it frightening. The only difference is that those that are comfortable don't see the wild as a place to be conquered and tamed. They accept things as they are and confidently and carefully move forward without fear. The ones unafraid of the wilderness know the rules and follow them.

Our journey toward a more just world is like moving through the wilderness. Our progress toward justice requires that we be unafraid, and all we need is to prepare ourselves and follow the rules. However, sometimes we just don't have all the rules to achieve justice. This is why sometimes we get burned out, experience depression, distrust each other, and battle each other. Howard Thurman warns us that walking into the wilderness of justice without internal preparation will lead us to moral fatigue. The persistent assaults on our collective psyche from racism, sexism, and homophobia require a deeper moral compass that gives us the calm confidence in our journey.

Thurman encourages us to "center down" and step out of the streets of our minds seething with endless traffic. Centering down is a way of being still in the wilderness. It allows us to ask questions about who we are, where we are going, and how we are going to get there. The four pivots in this book stand as the moral and ethical architecture for future movement building. Each of these pivots helps us recalibrate our collective compass toward justice in the wilderness of life. Social transformation requires both social and personal engagement. Justice is not only an outside game that comes from marches, rallies, and legal victories. It is also an inside game that requires that we cultivate spaces of solitude, reflection, and vision. We just need to make these four pivots in this book to be at one with the wilderness and ultimately find our way. So how will you choose to be still in the wild? What will you do to step out of the traffic of life and center down?

## DANCING BETWEEN ACCOUNTABILITY AND GRACE

Being still in the wild requires both accountability and grace. For the most part, we progressives are really good at accountability but not so good about grace. We know how to hold others accountable when they intentionally inflict harm and suffering on the communities we care about. We also know how to hold ourselves accountable when members of our own group fall short of our ideals for justice. Accountability is a necessary requirement for justice, and it allows us to force people, institutions, and laws to respond in ways that meet the needs of the collective good. Grace on the other hand is entirely different, and we have to work harder to practice it. *Grace is giving ourselves and others undeserved permission to be human.* It's hard to practice grace when you're afraid your family may be deported or fear you'll be fired because you complained about sexual harassment. It's hard to practice grace with others if we first don't practice it with ourselves.

Perhaps more than anything else, these four pivots require each of us to joyfully dance between accountability and grace, a type of letting go of all the little things that we sweat over. Forgetting your friend's birthday, always being late to meetings, yelling at your child, failing to send out the email when you said you would are things that make us say, "I could just kick myself." But this is not grace, and we have to learn that grace is something we give ourselves and others when it's not deserved. Grace is a reckoning with mercy, and time after time I've learned that it is the only way to walk through the wilderness toward justice.

Dancing between accountability and grace is an art form. *Without grace, accountability becomes social confinement, and without accountability, grace can become sentimental surrender.* We need to joyfully dance between both, and when this happens, we collectively humanize one another and create new ways of being together, and we come to realize that the wilderness is not so scary as we believed. We need to be human with each other, and I need others to see me as human. This is the only way that our movements for justice will evolve, when we collectively turn inward to heal our hearts and soothe our souls. It's not an easy dance, but it's a worthy one.

Grace Lee Boggs reminds us that over her years of addressing the harm done to workers, people of color, Indigenous peoples, women, gays and lesbians, and the disabled, she's seen a dark side in our work that leads us to "think of ourselves more as 'determined' than as 'self-determined,' more as victims of 'isms' (racism, sexism, capitalism, ableism) than as human beings who have the power of choice" to thrive in our efforts to create a more just society. "For our own survival we must assume individual and collective responsibility for creating a new nation. . . . Each of us needs to undergo a tremendous philosophical and spiritual transformation."[1]

In our dance through the wilderness, we come to realize that transformative justice is not so much about left or right politics, progressive or conservative policies, nor red and blue states. These are the old binary political configurations that keep us lost in the woods, circling without a map of where to go. There is a third way, and it's neither left nor right but up! The third way is an evolution in collective consciousness that transforms how we relate, interact, work, and play together. In our journey to create a more just world, all of us must learn to be more human and lean into the courage to create a world based in love and justice. Now let's go into the wild, together without fear, knowing that collectively we are destined to find that there was never a wilderness at all.

# NOTES

## Introduction

1 Loretta Ross, "I'm a Black Feminist. I Think Call-Out Culture Is Toxic," *New York Times*, August 17, 2019, https://www.nytimes .com/2019/08/17/opinion/sunday/cancel-culture-call-out.html.

2 Anthony A. Braga et al., "The Effects of Body-Worn Cameras on Police Activity and Police-Citizen Encounters," *Journal of Criminal Law and Criminology* 108, no. 3 (2018), https://scholarlycommons .law.northwestern.edu/jclc/vol108/iss3/3.

## Chapter 1

1 Lee Edward Colston II, "The Problem with Being 'Twice as Good,'" Medium, August 29, 2018, https://medium.com/@Mr.Write /the-problem-with-being-twice-as-good-1de095dcacee.

2 Brené Brown, *Dare to Lead: Brave Work, Tough Conversations, Whole Hearts* (New York: Random House, 2018), 112.

3 Cheryl Staats, Kelly Capatosto, Robin A. Wright, and Victoria W. Jackson, *State of the Science: Implicit Bias Review* (Kirwan Institute, 2016), http://kirwaninstitute.osu.edu/implicit-bias-training /resources/2015-implicit-bias-review.pdf.

4 Krista Tippett, "Ruby Sales: Where Does It Hurt?," January 16, 2020, in *On Being with Krista Tippett*, podcast, 52:09, https://onbeing .org/programs/ruby-sales-where-does-it-hurt/#transcript.

5 Roy F. Baumeister et al., "Bad Is Stronger Than Good," *Review of General Psychology* 5, no. 4 (2001), https://doi.org/10.1037%2F1089 -2680.5.4.323.

6 Julia A. Weiler, Boris Suchan, and Irene Daum, "When the Future Becomes the Past: Differences in Brain Activation Patterns for Episodic Memory and Episodic Future Thinking," *Behavioural Brain Research* 212, no. 2 (2010), https://doi.org/10.1016/j.bbr.2010.04.013.

7    Grace Lee Boggs and Scott Kurashige, *The Next American Revolution: Sustainable Activism for the Twenty-First Century* (Berkeley: University of California Press, 2011).

## Chapter 2

1    Matthew Lupoli, Lily Jampol, and Christopher Oveis, "Lying Because We Care: Compassion Increases Prosocial Lying," *Journal of Experimental Psychology* 146, no. 7 (2017): 1026–42, https://doi .org/10.1037/xge0000315.
2    Anita E. Kelly and Lijuan Wang, "A Life without Lies: Can Living More Honestly Improve Health" (paper presented at the APA Annual Convention, Orlando, FL, August 2012).

## Chapter 3

1    Aniruddha Das, "How Does Race Get 'Under the Skin'? Inflammation, Weathering, and Metabolic Problems in Late Life," *Social Science & Medicine* 77 (2013): 75–83, https://doi.org/10.1016/j .socscimed.2012.11.007.

## Chapter 4

1    John H. Bodley, *Cultural Anthropology: Tribes, States, and the Global System* (Lanham, MD: Rowman Altamira, 2011).
2    Pascal Molenberghs, "The Neuroscience of In-Group Bias," *Neuroscience & Biobehavioral Reviews* 37, no. 8 (2013), https://doi.org/10 .1016/j.neubiorev.2013.06.002.
3    Bastian Schiller, Thomas Baumgartner, and Daria Knoch, "Intergroup Bias in Third-Party Punishment Stems from Both Ingroup Favoritism and Outgroup Discrimination," *Evolution and Human Behavior* 35, no. 3 (2014): 169–75, https://doi.org/10.1016/j.evol humbehav.2013.12.006.
4    Jillian J. Jordan, Katherine McAuliffe, and Felix Warneken, "Development of In-Group Favoritism in Children's Third-Party Punishment of Selfishness," *Proceedings of the National Academy of Sciences* 111, no. 35 (2014): 12710–15, https://doi.org/10.1073 /pnas.1402280111.
5    Simone I. Flynn, "Social Movement Theory: Resource Mobilization Theory—Research Starters Sociology," EBSCO, 2009, http://www. academicpub.com/map/items/29755.html.

6   Howard Thurman, *A Strange Freedom: The Best of Howard Thur-man on Religious Experience and Public Life*, ed. Walter E. Fluker and Catherine Tumber (Boston: Beacon Press, 1998).

## Chapter 5

1   Jennifer S. Mascaro et al., "Compassion Meditation Enhances Empathic Accuracy and Related Neural Activity," *Social Cognitive and Affective Neuroscience* 8, no. 1 (2013): 48–55, https://doi.org/10.1093/scan/nss095.

2   Matthew D. Lieberman, *Social: Why Our Brains Are Wired to Connect* (Oxford, UK: Oxford University Press, 2013).

3   "Hardwired for Connection," PsychCare, 2016, accessed September 14, 2020, https://psychcaremd.com/hardwired-for-connection/.

4   Bishop Desmond Tutu, *No Future without Forgiveness* (New York: Doubleday, 1999), 125.

5   "Constitution of the Republic of South Africa, Act 200 of 1993," Government of South Africa, https://www.gov.za/documents/constitution/constitution-republic-south-africa-act-200-1993.

## Chapter 6

1   Brené Brown, *Daring Greatly: How the Courage to Be Vulnerable Transforms the Way We Live, Love, Parent, and Lead* (New York: Gotham Books, 2012).

## Chapter 8

1   Robin D. G. Kelley, *Freedom Dreams: The Black Radical Imagination* (Boston: Beacon Press, 2002), 11–12.

2   Kelley, *Freedom Dreams*, 14.

## Chapter 10

1   David Matthews, "Capitalism and Mental Health," *Monthly Review* 70, no. 8 (2019), https://monthlyreview.org/2019/01/01/capitalism-and-mental-health/.

2   Mihaly Csikszentmihalyi, *Flow: The Psychology of Optimal Experience* (New York: Harper & Row, 1990).

3   John Eligon, "They Push. They Protest. And Many Activists, Privately, Suffer as a Result," *New York Times*, March 28, 2018, https://www.nytimes.com/2018/03/26/us/they-push-they-protest -and-many-activists-privately-suffer-as-a-result.html.

4   Yashna Maya Padamsee, "Communities of Care, Organizations for Liberation," 2016, https://nayamaya.wordpress.com/2011/06/19 /communities-of-care-organizations-for-liberation/.

5   Thomas Merton, *Conjectures of a Guilty Bystander* (New York: Doubleday, 1966), 73.

## Chapter 11

1   Alice M. Gregory et al., "Dysfunctional Beliefs and Attitudes about Sleep in Children," *Journal of Sleep Research* 18, no. 4 (2009): 422–26, https://doi.org/10.1111/j.1365-2869.2009.00747.x.

2   Arianna Huffington, *The Sleep Revolution: Transforming Your Life, One Night at a Time*, pbk ed. (New York: Harmony Books, 2017), 20.

3   Terrie Williams, *Black Pain: It Just Looks Like We're Not Hurting: Real Talk for When There's Nowhere to Go but Up* (New York: Scribner, 2008), 31.

4   Damon Young, "I Pray for Murder (Sometimes): I've Learned How to Dodge a Bullet. But How Do You Dodge a Stroke?" *New York Times*, September 28, 2019, https://www.nytimes.com/2019/09/28 /opinion/sunday/black-men-murder-death.html.

5   Dayna A. Johnson et al., "Are Sleep Patterns Influenced by Race/ Ethnicity—a Marker of Relative Advantage or Disadvantage? Evidence to Date," *Nature and Science of Sleep* 11 (2019): 79–95, https://doi.org/10.2147%2FNSS.S169312.

6   Xiaoli Chen et al., "Racial/Ethnic Differences in Sleep Disturbances: The Multi-Ethnic Study of Atherosclerosis (MESA)," *Sleep* 38, no. 6 (June 2015): 877–88, https://doi.org/10.5665/sleep.4732.

7   Kelin Li and Ming Wen, "Racial and Ethnic Disparities in Leisure-Time Physical Activity in California: Patterns and Mechanisms," *Race and Social Problems* 5, no. 3 (2013): 147–56, https://doi.org /10.1007/s12552-013-9087-9.

## Chapter 12

1   Boggs and Kurashige, *Next American Revolution,* 33.

# INDEX

# ABOUT THE AUTHOR

Photo credit: Bryon Malik @5malik

**Shawn Ginwright, PhD**, is one of the nation's leading innovators, provocateurs, and thought leaders on African American youth, youth activism, and youth development. He is a professor of education in the Africana Studies Department and a senior research associate at San Francisco State University. His research examines the ways in which youth in urban communities navigate through the constraints of poverty and struggle to create equality and justice in their schools and communities. Ginwright is the founder and chief executive officer of Flourish Agenda, Inc., a research lab and consulting firm whose mission is to design strategies that unlock the power of healing and engage youth of color and adult allies in transforming their schools and communities.

In 2011 he was awarded the prestigious Fulbright Senior Specialist award from the US State Department for his outstanding research and work with urban youth. He is the author of *Hope and Healing in Urban Education: How Urban Activists and Teachers Are Reclaiming Matters of the Heart, Black Youth Rising: Activism and Radical Healing in Urban America,* and *Black in School: Afrocentric Reform, Urban Youth, and the Promise of Hip-Hop Culture* and coeditor of *Beyond Resistance! Youth Activism and Community Change: New Democratic Possibilities for Practice and Policy for America's Youth.*

Dr. Ginwright served as chairman of the board for the California Endowment from 2018 to 2021, with oversight of a $3 billion endowment to improve the health of California's underserved communities. He also serves on the advisory board for the Center for Information & Research on Civic Learning at the Jonathan Tisch College of Civic Life at Tufts University. Ginwright lives in Oakland, California, with his lovely wife and is currently an empty-nester— both children are in college.

# *About North Atlantic Books*

North Atlantic Books (NAB) is a 501(c)(3) nonprofit publisher committed to a bold exploration of the relationships between mind, body, spirit, culture, and nature. Founded in 1974, NAB aims to nurture a holistic view of the arts, sciences, humanities, and healing. To make a donation or to learn more about our books, authors, events, and newsletter, please visit www.northatlanticbooks.com.